THE *Odyssey* OF A PURPLE HEART VET

THE BATTLE OF OKINAWA

By

JAMES BEVERLY WILLIS

ISBN-13

978-1-4991024-5-1

Cover and interior design
by
Alan McCuller/www.mc2graphics.com

Lone Star Productions

Printed in the United States of America

First Edition

Corporal James B. Willis
Company C, 77th Division
Purple Heart Veteran of World War II
Wounded in the Battle of Okinawa on June 17, 1945

TABLE OF CONTENTS

FOREWORD

This book focuses primarily on Okinawa, during the last and deadliest battle of the Pacific Theater of World War II. Stories and statistics concerning the war at other places during the Second World War have been inserted to relate a glimpse of what was happening with Americans in many places of the world during that period of time. Much has been written by people who have had firsthand experiences, even frontline combat, in all theaters of that war. Hopefully, the reader will be inspired to select some of those writings to learn more of the supreme price that has been paid for freedom.

The thought of chronicling historical events in my lifetime and my own experiences during those times, is one that has continued to pursue me for a number of years. Here in the later years of my life, it is due time that I do so as a dedication to those who have passed before me and to those who follow.

While most were ordinary occurrences experienced by many of my generation, others have been quite extraordinary indeed. The period of history in which I have lived is a fascinating one, full of marvelous discoveries, as well as vast social and cultural changes. It would be impossible to touch upon all of them or even to recall here, the many turns my life has taken. Who else could relate these things? There is truth in the saying, that when a person dies a library of information is lost forever. Through God's mercy I have lived a full life, rich in meaningful experiences. What follows is a portion of my life's journey that I wish to put down in writing, in the hope it will benefit those who read this book. Fortunately, my memories have remained sharp and clear, as if they happened yesterday, enabling me to accomplish this.

The Battle of Okinawa is understandably one of the most vivid and memorable fragments of my life, even though it encompasses a brief window of time. The intention here is to give the reader a glimpse of what the war was like and the conditions the soldiers endured. Yet even today, I am reluctant to write about my military experience, because I wish not to glorify myself, nor the misery and destruction of war. For that very reason, throughout the years I have chosen to refrain from talking much about my war experiences. Only in the retelling of these battle stories does the sleeping wounds of war awaken my memory of the horrors of that time. I ask for neither praise nor sympathy for my role. God blessed me with a safe return to my homeland. Therefore, I trust the reader to appreciate this writing of my story in this light.

ACKNOWLEDGMENTS

As I look over my shoulder at these last few years of working long hours, writing my memoirs, and gathering material for this book, I'm amazed at how the Lord has sustained me with abundant energy and endurance to complete this task. There have been opportunities that I know He has provided. He has also provided the right people at the right time, which has been an awesome blessing.

I am especially thankful to my precious wife, Berline. She is my closest friend, advisor and supporter. Her encouragement has been most needed.

I would like to thank my children and extended family for their unwavering support of this effort. Among all of them, their broad range of talents from research, proofreading, revising, filing, to editing has made the project move smoothly.

My son, Alvin Eugene, provided his detailed hand-drawn illustrations. I wish to extend special thanks to him for depicting these scenes that otherwise would be impossible to have.

Author and teacher, Del Cain, helped me greatly with general book writing procedures. His latest published work is a collection of poetry entitled *Songs On the Prairie Wind*. He also directed me to a wonderful publisher by the name of Ginnie Siena Bivona. Her commitment to excellence has made my book possible to a world of readers.

Lisa Lasky of the Weithorn family graciously provided a photograph of my friend, Herbert Weithorn.

Finally, I am thankful to God for the blessing of a spared and long life that He has given me. It is my hope that my life, as well as this book, will bring honor and glory to Him. May you see the finger of God and be drawn to Him as you read…. *The Odyssey of a Purple Heart Vet*!

CHAPTER ONE

LEAVING THE NEST
A Fork in the Road

Europe was at war, but in the spring of 1941 it all seemed far away to a 16-year-old country boy about to graduate from high school. In fact, I was looking forward to my 17th birthday, only three days after the big event at Petersburg High School (PHS) in April. The school term in Pike County, Indiana, was only eight months at that time. It felt like I was stepping out of my childhood, spent in a small four-room farmhouse built by my father, onto a canvas of new adventures and carving out a future for myself. On April 23, 1924, I was the fourth of seven children born to Floyd and Inez Willis. We were a hardworking family, for there were always many chores to do on the farm. Our home was about four miles south of Petersburg, Indiana, the county seat. We lived in the small community called Clark's Station, which is now known as Willisville.

James Willis - high school graduation photo 1941

I had worked and saved my money, with which I bought the first suit I ever owned. It was teal green, purchased out of the Montgomery Ward mail order catalog. There was even enough in my savings to afford a new tie. It was a pretty fancy "getup" for a country boy used to wearing coveralls and hand-me-downs, and going barefoot all summer. I was happy to have appropriate attire for the occasion. Also, I knew Mom was pretty proud of the way I looked.

Toward the end of my high school year, I had been bombarded with invitations offering a variety of adventures and benefits. Colorful brochures and mailings came from industries, colleges, and certain branches of the military. All guaranteed me a bright, exciting, and prosperous future by joining them!! The invitations from the Marines and the U.S. Navy painted an especially glamorous story awaiting those who joined them.

As I studied attractive mailings from the military branches, I was giving serious consideration to the benefits of enlisting. Upon more reflection, however, I decided to further my education by attending college. That time of my life, I compare to the situation where one may be walking down a path in the woods and it comes to a divide. A decision has to be made as to which path should be taken. Without the assurance of the outcome, one has to consider many things about what to do. Often it seems best to take the path that shows more traffic!

Ultimately, I decided to attend the Purdue University School of Forestry. The only obstacle was money. College was expensive and there simply was no money at our house for that. If that plan was to be realized I would have to earn the necessary funds. Working most of the summer of 1941, painting houses with my brothers, I saved enough money to enroll for the fall classes.

At the time of registration, just two weeks before the beginning of school, I had accumulated sufficient funds to pay for the first semester tuition of $72. There was enough left for books and other small expenses. More funds would soon be needed to pay for housing and other miscellaneous expenses.

At the Office of Student Employment and Housing, I was informed of a part-time job where the manager was looking for a student interested in exchanging work for free lodging. The manager, Mr. Pierce, was very pleased with my application because of my painting experience. I was to share a large two-room apartment with four other fellows. We all slept in one room; the other housed our desks and shelves for study. My roommates included a wealthy boy from Italy, named Dara Secban, who allowed me to drive his 1942 DeSoto.

One was Charles Ember, a farmer. We had a lot in common and related easily to one another. Sometimes, the others were a bit confused by the slang and sayings we used. The other one was Tom Houchens, who was from a different background. It was a good friendly arrangement, even with our differences and the need to overlook occasional tendencies to be the "one in the know". But with good natured give and take, we lived without conflict.

Mr. Pierce and I painted rooms for two weeks before time for enrollment. After classes commenced, he needed me to work occasionally in a variety of ways. I assisted tenants as they were moving in or out. In order to meet my obligation to Mr. Pierce, I always tried to make myself available for that. I was usually rewarded with a lucrative tip for the service. In addition to that work assistance, Mr. Pierce would occasionally ask me to sit in his office to answer service calls if he had to be out for a while. That position was a real blessing and an answer to prayer, because it provided my lodging for the entire first year of school. Both his office and my apartment were very close to the Purdue campus. It was a pleasure to walk through the beautiful surroundings and to the various buildings on the grounds where I needed to attend class. I was too busy to think about the things back home or even get homesick. I was excited to be on my own and in a wholesome atmosphere.

Purdue: People and Plans

During the first year, the schedule was fairly well dictated. There were required basic courses for all freshmen students, allowing only one elective. The choices were entomology and botany, or the student could do both. Introductory Forestry, a non-credit but very interesting course, was one of the basic studies for forestry students. Math requirements for me were advanced algebra, followed by trigonometry the second semester. Math, always my favorite subject, meant that those were my most enjoyed classes. In fact, I had graduated from high school with the highest math grades of anyone in my class. Biology was required and took considerable study time, but I liked learning the material. The one class I did not enjoy was a speech class. Being very shy, I felt awkward when speaking before groups. Still, I managed to get a passing grade.

All male students were required to take Reserve Officer Training Course (ROTC) and were furnished regular military uniforms. The ROTC class was a field artillery training course, which met twice each week. We were required to wear the uniform to class, but in reality it was necessary to wear them all day, because we didn't have time to change between classes. During that class, we were taught military rules and instructions on the use of artillery weapons. At the age of 17 I had not begun to shave yet, but I had a little whisker fuzz on my face. On the second day of class the sergeant gave me orders, "Willis, get that fuzz off your face before the next class."

I went out that evening to invest in shaving equipment for the first time in my life.

Activity on the campus was alive with students going to various buildings for classes. I wondered why all those students were so friendly with a country kid like me. I soon learned that many of those students came from the country with a background similar to mine. The friendly greetings, from passing students walking across campus, made it easy to meet new friends. Many of those country kids, away from home, were also eager to have companionship.

One of the forestry students became a close friend and invited me to his room one day. He was wearing a cross, which I had not noticed before, hanging from a chain around his neck. I asked him the meaning of it. He replied, "I wear that all the time so that if I get killed the priest can pray me into heaven."

I had never heard of such a thing and gave him a little sermon. I explained to him that was not true, because a priest could not pray anyone into Heaven. I went on to say that he needed to pray for himself and accept salvation while he is living, in order to go to Heaven. He didn't seem to accept my belief any more than I accepted the meaning of his cross. However, we remained good friends while we were at Purdue attending most of the same classes together.

Work Ethics Pay Off

I needed to get another part-time job in order to meet additional expenses, as previously mentioned. Upon checking with the student employment office, I learned there was a job at a restaurant conveniently located near the apartment building where I was living. They were hiring a few students at the regular student rate of 25 cents per hour. My job there was to clear away the dishes and clean the tables when people were finished eating.

Surprisingly, that job turned out to be very disturbing to me. It was not that the work was hard, it was the enormous waste of food that offended me. I was a farm boy from a poor home in a rather underprivileged community. At home we did not waste anything, especially not food! Each time I went to work and cleared those tables, I watched perfectly good food being thrown into the garbage. Workers were not permitted to salvage any of that food, touched or not! To further my distress, we had to pay full price for anything on the menu that we wanted to eat. I was frankly astonished at the fancy restaurant having, which seemed to me, astronomical prices. With their unreasonable prices it was not a place at which I could afford to eat. Although restaurants may have been required to treat leftover food in that manner, the seeming disregard for the philosophy of "waste not, want not" continued to grate on my ingrained set of principles and values. At any rate, working there about two hours each day was a way of making enough money to provide for my basic needs.

After enduring that unpleasant job for a short while, Mr. Pierce approached me with an opportunity to work for a locker plant. He said, "Jim, Mr. Gould owns a locker plant just one block from here. He is looking to find someone for evening part-time work. Would you be interested?" I replied that it certainly would be better than the restaurant job.

He explained that the locker plant was a meat processing business. Because of his approval of my work ethic and production, he felt confident to give me a good recommendation. He gave the location and told me to speak with the manager, Tom Gould. Mr. Pierce explained, "I have spoken to Mr. Gould, and he is expecting you to come over to see him." I considered that an added blessing and a reward for being a diligent worker.

Without delay I went to see about the new job. Mr. Gould met me in a very friendly manner. After I introduced myself, he said, "Mr. Pierce says you might be interested in a part-time job."

I replied, "Yes, he told me that you would be expecting me."

Mr. Gould said, "This is an evening job and I would need you here for about three hours each evening to help put up orders, which would involve some meat cutting." He went on to ask, "Have you had any experience like that?"

"Well," I replied, "I have helped my dad butcher hogs. I've skinned rabbits, cleaned fish, and helped Mom dress chickens. Does that qualify?"

He laughed about that and said, "That's good enough to suit me. If you can be here tomorrow about 7 pm, the evening worker, George, will show you what to do. And from now on you can just call me Tom."

It was an evening job that paid the same standard student wage of 25 cents per hour, but he gave me more hours. It was also a better fit with my daily class schedule. The job was from three to four hours each evening and after my Saturday morning classes. In those days many colleges had Saturday morning classes. At Purdue we were required to have at least one Saturday morning class. I scheduled the earliest class possible so I could report for work in good time. By earning $6 to $8 each week, I could easily save enough for my second semester. Tuition had increased to a phenomenal cost of $74, the extra $2 was because of a lab fee.

The job at the locker plant proved to be a good move. I liked the job of unloading and processing sides and quarters of meat. In addition, the meat-cutting manager of the processing room trained me to be a meat cutter. I learned the process of cutting those slabs of meat into steaks, grinding hamburger, cutting bacon, and filling orders for restaurants and college boarding houses. Some of the orders called for 100 servings or more of whatever was to be served the next day. After orders were completed on Tuesday night, we usually had to wait for the delivery truck to arrive from Chicago with a supply of pork and beef quarters and containers of other meat products to be unloaded. On those nights it would be 11 pm or midnight before we would finish. We even got paid for the time we waited. When orders were slack on Saturday, one or two of us would have to work in the deep freeze to organize and arrange the frozen supplies. We went prepared with coat, cap, and gloves for working in that zero-degree room.

An extra benefit of that job was I could buy cheese and lunchmeat for making sandwiches at a discounted price. In addition, I had learned a new skill and trade in the process. Mr. Gould was very pleased with my work and thought I had a good attitude towards work. He would, on occasion, give me a small package of some goodies to take home as an extra bonus. I felt it was a reward for being a dependable worker. Altogether, the job proved to be a real blessing to me. I believe that it came as a result of my faith in the Lord and trusting Him to provide for my needs.

Floyd and Inez Willis family home in Clark's Station, now known as Willisville, Indiana [M. Crabtree drawing]

After six weeks of school and the two weeks of work prior, I had been away from home for eight weeks. That was the longest time I had ever been away. I was beginning to get homesick, but the limited time to get home after Saturday class and make it back for Monday class didn't allow much time for the 150-mile trip each way. That was especially true because I would have to hitchhike. It meant getting out on the road, holding out my thumb, and hoping some kind soul would give me a ride down the road. Finally, I decided to give it a try even if it meant getting back late on Sunday. One Saturday Mr. Gould gave me permission to be off work. As soon as my class was over at nine o'clock that morning, I wasted no time getting out of town to catch a ride. Many people were willing to pick up students that were dressed respectably and I soon caught my first ride. To my pleasant surprise I actually made it home by about four in the evening. It was a joyful time all around getting back home and seeing all the family, who were very happy to see me. There was so much to tell!

However, there was a piece of bad news too. In the summer before leaving for Purdue, I had raised a nice flock of 15 to 20 white ducks. They ranged in size from two weeks old to half-grown ducks. I had kept the smaller ones in pens. They could not be allowed to go to the canal behind our home, because the large turtles there could catch them by the foot and eat them. The larger ducks could survive on the canal without getting caught by the turtles. After I left, no one wanted the job of feeding and watering the penned up ducks. They were turned loose, and naturally went to the canal with the bigger ducks. I was sad to learn that most of my ducks did not survive.

By noon on Sunday I was back catching rides on my way to Lafayette, arriving at the apartment by 6 pm. After the success of that first trip home, I felt confident to make more frequent trips, which I did about every four or five weeks.

That refreshing visit with home folks, as well as the success of hitchhiking there and back, gave me a burst of enthusiasm. I returned, eager to be back at school attending classes and working at the locker plant each evening. What an adventure all of the new life at Purdue was for me! After a few weeks, something of a regular routine was established. It went like this: Up early in time for a stop at the small restaurant across the street for a cheap breakfast, on to my eight o'clock class, a little study time between classes, try to grab a late lunch somewhere, and then (time permitting) go back to my room before needing to be at the locker plant by 7 pm. All in all, college life was an interesting experience, even if I did have to work part time. I really think the work made it even more interesting.

Pearl Harbor Day

In addition to the other chores that paid for my room rent in the Varsity Apartments, I tended the office for Mr. Pierce, the manager, when he had to be away for an extended period of time. I liked that because it gave me an opportunity to accomplish my school work in a quiet environment.

One Sunday afternoon, as I was sitting in the office studying, Mr. Pierce and his wife returned from their afternoon drive. He asked me, "Jim have you heard the news?"

"No," I replied, "I have been busy studying and haven't turned on the radio." (There was no such thing as television at that time.) He announced the news, "Japan bombed Pearl Harbor this morning!"

The surprise had been complete! Two waves of planes attacked, dropping bombs and torpedoes. The first wave of 168 planes hit its target at 7:53 am. The second wave of 170 planes hit at 8:55. By 9:55 it was all over. By 1 pm, the six carriers that launched the planes, from 274 miles off the coast of Oahu, were heading back to Japan.

PEARL HARBOR
ATTACKED

trouble. Its pocket battleships were not as large as other battleships, but could travel faster. In December, 1939, a British naval force in the South Atlantic cornered a pocket battleship, the *Admiral Graf Spee*, and damaged it. The German warship took refuge in Montevideo harbor, where its captain scuttled it on Hitler's order and committed suicide.

On Jan. 30, 1941, the Germans announced that ships of any nationality taking aid to Britain would be torpedoed. Rear Adm. Karl Doenitz, commander of the German submarine fleet, devised "wolf-pack" tactics for attacking Allied shipping. His U-boats operated in groups of about 8 or 9, and sometimes as many as 20.

German, Italian, and Japanese firms in Latin America.

Relations between Japan and the United States became increasingly tense in the fall of 1941, when a new Japanese cabinet took office. Lt. Gen. Hideki Tojo, leader of the extremist Japanese military group, became premier. His cabinet immediately began planning for war with the United States. Tojo sent a special representative, Saburo Kurusu, to help Ambassador Kichisaburo Nomura negotiate with Secretary of State Cordell Hull. The two countries argued over American aid to China, the Japanese troops in Indochina, Japan's frozen assets, and its exploitation of resources in the Netherlands East Indies. Late in November, the Japa-

Behind them was left chaos; 2,403 dead, 188 destroyed planes and a crippled American Pacific Fleet that included 8 damaged or destroyed battleships. The Japanese lost only 29 aircraft. In that one stroke, the Japanese action ended the debate over entering the war that had divided Americans ever since the German defeat of France.

Approximately three hours later, Japanese planes began a day-long attack on American facilities in the Philippines. Because the islands are located across the International Dateline, the local Philippine time was just after 5 am on December 8. Farther to the west, the Japanese struck at Hong Kong, Malaysia, and Thailand. That was a coordinated attempt to use surprise attacks on strategic targets in order to inflict as much damage as possible.

The Attack on Pearl Harbor on Dec. 7, 1941, plunged the United States into war. Japanese aircraft sank 18 ships and killed or wounded 3,681 persons. President Franklin D. Roosevelt signed the declaration of war.

The day after the assault, President Franklin D. Roosevelt asked Congress to declare war on Japan. Congress approved his declaration with just one dissenting vote. Three days later the Japanese allies, Germany and Italy, declared war on the United States. Once again Congress reciprocated. More than two years into the international conflict, America had finally joined World War II. [From United States Military Archives and Wikipedia, the Free Encyclopedia]

The bombing of Pearl Harbor was a complete surprise to us. That fateful day of December 7, 1941, is still remembered as a day of horrible disaster in the minds of those living at the time. The unprovoked attack by the Japanese is recorded in history as a *Day of Infamy* for the world to remember.

There was no escaping the thought that I was just about the right age for the draft. At some time in the near future, I would likely be called up and my college work interrupted. I would remain in school until that time came. Providentially, I was spared some time before being called.

By working so many hours it was difficult to find time to study sufficiently. Nevertheless, I managed to get through the first year with passing grades and excelled in trigonometry class the second semester. My successful courses in algebra and geometry played an important factor in my joy of trigonometry. We had an outstanding teacher who expected us to come to class prepared with completed lessons, tools, and with our book ready to continue learning.

Toward the end of the 1942 school year, all students in the School of Forestry were offered an opportunity to apply for summer employment with the National Forest Service. The job paid 70 cents per hour, which was more than most labor jobs at 50 cents an hour. I eagerly signed up and waited for my work assignment. It wasn't long until I received word that I was to report to a firefighting camp in Missoula, Montana, that summer on June 15. It would be only two weeks after school was out. I would have approximately one week to go home and prepare to travel. What a feeling of excitement and adventure–I was going out west!

The War Develops

Up to that time, we had been learning of some serious things that were happening in the war. News did not travel as fast as today, so we weren't able to get the full impact of how the war was developing. News commentators could not get close to the real events, but we did hear that the Japanese were making advances in what became known as the Pacific Theater. As time went on, we learned of the severity of the Japanese attacks.

In the latter part of December 1941, the Japanese invaded the Philippines. The United States Army and the Philippine soldiers tried to resist the invasion, but had neither sufficient training nor the necessary equipment and manpower to hold out against the Japanese. Eventually, in March 1942, about 80,000 Philippine and American soldiers and Philippine civilians were captured at Mariveles, at the tip of the Bataan Peninsula.

The Japanese took them all as prisoners and began what became known as the *Bataan Death March*. It was a grueling 60-mile march across the entire length of the Bataan Peninsula from Mariveles to San Fernando. There the survivors of the march were loaded on trucks and rail cars to be sent to Camp O'Donnell. The Japanese were extremely cruel and inhumane, treating them like animals. Over 5,000 of them died or were killed on that march. Hundreds more died (while interned as Japanese POW's) by starvation, disease, and punishment. That amounted to a war crime by the Japanese. Because of that, some of the leaders were tried and executed after the war.

CHAPTER TWO

MONTANA FORESTRY VENTURE

Chance of a Lifetime

The United States began drafting 18-year-old boys for military training because they did not have enough enlisted men. I was only 17 years of age at the time. I figured that I would not be drafted for at least a few months and could continue right on with school.

After my last day of classes for the school term at Purdue, I gathered my few belongings and hitchhiked home to prepare for my journey to Montana. The only preparation I had to do was assemble some necessary items in a traveling bag and study some road maps. I needed to determine the best route to take. Public transportation was rather expensive so I decided to hitchhike the 2,000 miles to Missoula. Mom and Pop thought it was too much for me to hitchhike that far, but with the typical optimism of youth I had no doubts about it. I was to learn that cross-country hitchhiking may not be entirely uneventful!

On a Monday morning I left home with one small travel bag and $50 in my pocket. I arrived at the National Forest Headquarters in Missoula in less than a week.

Some of the people I met along the way were almost as interesting as the landscape, especially the ones who gave me rides. One generous guy picked me up in the evening, he drove all night, and the next morning he took me to his home for breakfast. After breakfast, he drove me out to the edge of town so I could catch my next ride.

Another night I had a very frightening, life threatening experience. A man had let me off, late into the evening, at a "road house" (a tavern of ill repute and a den for dubious activities such as heavy drinking, gambling, and more) far out in the country. It was a place with little to no traffic. I had waited beside the road for two hours for a possible ride. At length three guys came reeling out of the road house and stopped to offer me a ride. Reluctantly, because I knew they had been drinking, I got into the car. The need to get to a better location overrode my better judgment. I thought that, just maybe, they would get me at least a few miles further to the edge of the next town where I could ask to be let off and try for a different ride.

Too late, I realized that all three of them were very drunk and the driver was driving dangerously fast. I watched in terror, as I saw him fast approaching an old Model-T

Ford that was just creeping slowly along. When I saw that he was not slowing for it, I yelled at him, "There's a car in front of you!" He swerved to miss the Ford and almost lost control. Struggling to stay on the road, he finally came to a halt crossways! We had stopped on a long bridge across a river.

I saw my chance and I took it! Grabbing my handbag I quickly leaped out of that car. Sprinting back to the rickety old car we had nearly flattened, I asked the driver if I could possibly ride ahead into the next town with him.

The man acted really scared! His terrified expression caused me to realize that he might think it was a hold up or something. Here a car had just sped past him and blocked his way. Now, one of the passengers came running back toward him!

Quickly I explained, "That is a drunk driver! He almost rear-ended your car causing a bad wreck, if I had not been along to yell at him. I think that I saved the lives of all of us!" Then, I asked, "May I ride to the next town with you?" "Climb in young man," he replied, "You are welcome!"

The drunk driver of the Chevy managed to get his car straightened back up on the road and hit the gas. Now that the road was unblocked, I rode safely on with the man in the old open top Ford the short distance into the next town. There I got a room for the night.

The remainder of the way to Missoula was relatively uneventful. I arrived on Friday at noon and reported immediately to the National Forest Headquarters, as instructed. After getting signed in, I had time to shop for some logging boots and other recommended supplies. After the five-day trip, I had only $20 remaining from the $50 I started with. That was enough to buy the needed items. Other guys, from various colleges all over the country, had also arrived at the Forestry office. Late in the afternoon a forest ranger took us 40 miles, by truck, to a camp that was nine miles north of the little town of Huson.

It was named *Nine Mile Camp* and was located there as a forest firefighting camp. Even though it was the middle of June, the barracks were uncomfortably cold. We were thankful to see a stove standing there, in the middle of the large room. We built a fire for some heat and got settled in. I had arrived at my destination. The Lord had blessed and protected me with a safe, interesting, and affordable trip.

There were 100 guys who arrived at the camp from different colleges around the United States. We were divided into four crews, with twenty-five in each group, living in four separate barracks. Life was very interesting at the forest camp. Our supervisor warned about not feeding the bears and to be especially cautious if we saw a bear with cubs. We were taught the methods of fighting forest fires. Each crew had two men assigned to run the cross-cut saw, for cutting trees or logs. Several wanted that assignment, so the foreman had each one to demonstrate their abilities. I was quite experienced with that type of saw, because as a boy I had used it repeatedly when helping out an elderly neighbor.

When the foreman saw that I was experienced with it, he put me on the opposite end from some of the men being tested, so I could give them pointers on the correct technique. Needless to say, I was assigned to the cross-cut job. When fighting fires, I enjoyed running the saw much more than digging trenches or other jobs.

We also worked at making hay for the mules. Mules ran wild on the open range. Some of those were occasionally rounded up and brought to the ranch for training. The mules did not take lightly to that restriction and training. One day, while I was at the ranch, I observed the rangers working with the wild mules, training them for packing supplies. It was a new experience for me. Those mules had a definite opinion about it. The fits they threw left no doubt of their displeasure at being controlled. After the mules were broken, they were used in mule trains to carry supplies into the forests. A mule train consisted of nine or ten mules, all in a single file with a lead strap to each. The "train" was led by a man on a saddle horse.

One day our crew climbed to the top of a peak 4,000 feet high. That was to help condition us for hiking in the mountains and to get accustomed to high altitudes. On five different occasions, we were called upon to fight fires during that summer.

One night, around midnight, the whole crew was called out to prepare for a long trip to a fire in Yellowstone National Park where two separate fires were burning.

The kitchen had made sack lunches so we could eat breakfast on the way. We all loaded on the back of camp trucks and were taken to Missoula. There, two Greyhound buses awaited us for the trip to Yellowstone. Traveling all night, we finally arrived at the park the following morning. Open-topped sightseeing park buses were waiting there to take us to the area of the fire. I thought they would rush us out there as fast as possible, but they explained that we could not do much with the fire until later in the evening or early in the morning. That allowed time for the buses to take us past all the sightseeing places on the way. They even stopped occasionally for us to snap some pictures.

From the point where we got off the buses, we hiked quite a distance through the forest. It was afternoon when we arrived at the fire area. The mule train, carrying supplies, followed. They arrived in time for us to have the necessary tools to work on the fire trenches before nightfall. When it became dark it was time to bed down, in our sleeping bags, at a safe distance from the fire. The camp leader woke us up at four o'clock each morning. After bathing in ice-cold water from the mountain stream, we had breakfast at the field kitchen. Then we filed out, following the leader to where we would get an early start at controlling the smoldering fire. That was the usual process when fighting a fire. Our crew of 100 ambitious guys had that fire under control in four days. We then packed up our sleeping bags and hiked out to the road, where it looked like civilization again.

The park service brought a convoy of sightseeing buses and took us around the southern part of the park, past all of the interesting spots along the way toward the destination of another fire on the east side of the park. We were taken by truck, through a jungle of trees and over ditches for three miles. From that point we hiked another three miles to the area of the fire. Once again, a mule train carried supplies to our campsite. It took three days to get that fire under control. The remnants of both fires were left for the mop-up crews of the park service.

On the way back, the park buses gave us a tour past different interesting sights, then we were taken to a hotel at the north entrance of the park. How good to bathe, shave, clean up, have a good meal, and sleep in a nice clean comfortable bed again. To us, it was like a luxury hotel and a real treat after living in the wilderness for over a week. What a genuine blessing!

Early the next morning we boarded a train to take us back to Missoula. It was a relaxing ride, viewing the spectacular mountain forest along the way. We were served a nice lunch on the train. Approaching Missoula, we could see a fire on a mountain slope some distance to the east of us and we discussed it among ourselves.

Although we were anxious to get back to camp, we expected that fire would probably be our next destination. Sure enough! The forest service trucks were there waiting for us, with the tools we would need to fight the fire. Immediately they took all of us to the fire area to start digging a trench ahead of the fire, with the the hopes of stopping it before morning. Fortunately, a rain came during the early hours of the morning and quenched the fire. We weary fire fighters were wet and cold, but glad the fire was out. Now we could be taken back to Nine Mile Camp. They let us rest all the next day and gave us the day off with pay. The time spent fighting fires seemed like good conditioning for combat readiness.

My summer at the forest camp was a very memorable and valuable experience in outdoor living, working, and spending time with other young men who, for the most part, had a common interest in working with nature and getting an education. However, not many of the guys were inclined to spiritual matters. There were no church services or other opportunities for even a Bible study. During the evening, after our day's activity I would often slip away into the forest among the trees surrounding the camp area. A log became my chair and altar for Scripture reading and prayer. There I could kneel and give thanks to God for His many blessings and pray for the well-being of my family back home. Due to the absence of a church that also served as the place for my Sunday morning worship.

On one such occasion, the Lord impressed upon me that my family might be in need of some money. Times were still financially difficult at home because the family depended on the meager income that Pop made working for the WPA (the Works Project Administration started by President Roosevelt). I frequently corresponded with the family, so the next day I put a 10-dollar bill in with my letter. I learned later that the family was working in the potato patch when the letter arrived. The money was indeed badly needed and was a blessing to them. I heard that when Mom received the money, she immediately sent someone to the grocery store to get some much needed food for lunch.

Some of us decided to build a dam across a nearby creek. We used large rocks from the bottom of the creek to make a swimming pool. The water was really cold, coming from high in the mountains, but it was refreshing to take a dip after a day of work (in the field making hay or hiking in the forest). There was a wash house for us to do our laundry but some guys took their laundry to the creek. Our white things began to look rather dingy by the end of our camp season because we were not experienced at laundering.

Besides working and fighting fires, the college age boys thought up some activities of their own. One such sort of fun was concocted when some of them decided to catch a bear. We had been seeing a bear make his rounds to the kitchen garbage can each evening. As they plotted and made their plan, they talked about how exciting it would be to see what the bear would do. I wondered to myself if they had given any thought to what they would do with the bear if they actually caught him. The guys borrowed a rope from the supply and fixed a lasso around the top of the garbage barrel where the bear came without fail to feast of its contents. When the rope was secured to their satisfaction, they hid in a nearby building to await the appearance of the bear at his usual time. Excitement began to mount when the unsuspecting bear came lumbering along. He got his body halfway down in the barrel to reach choice morsels. Then they gave a swift, strong pull on the rope! The rope slipped over the bear's head, catching only a front leg. As the noose tightened on it, the guys clung to the rope strengthening their grip. The furious bear put on quite a show, jumping, growling, and throwing a fit trying to get loose.

It was great fun for the whole camp to watch the daring sport from a distance! After they had enough entertainment they suddenly realized they had a slight problem. How were they and the rope to part ways with the bear? The guys did not want to just let the bear run off with the rope because it wasn't theirs. They would have to pay for it, so they held on. The bear managed to get a little slack in the rope, climbed up a large post, and stood there with all four feet on top of the post. At that juncture, it was a standoff between bear and rope holders. Finally, the bear got the rope off his foot and escaped into the forest.

Our days at Nine Mile Camp were always filled with activity and excitement. Another example was when in the open field, we could watch the smoke jumpers practice parachuting from their plane. On one occasion, we became alarmed upon seeing a jumper continue to fall without his parachute opening! We watched in horror as he fell halfway to the ground before it opened up. What a relief! We had feared that we were going to see a man fall to his death right before our very eyes.

Some of us were also given a chance to drive the antiquated hay trucks when making hay. Not having many chances to drive vehicles in my life, I loved getting to do that.

Participation in the numerous projects and requirements at the camp, along with some astonishing occurrences, made it one of the most thrilling and rewarding adventures of my life. It all resulted from having enrolled in the School of Forestry at Purdue. Little did I realize how the training there would be of help to me in the days ahead.

By the end of our assignment, all of us were ready to get back to civilization and gear up for school. Of course, that work experience was part of our ultimate goal in preparing for a vocation in life. The things I learned there served to increase my conviction that I had made the right choice of a career in forestry.

The student jobs with the Forest Service ended late in August, allowing time for us to make it back for the beginning of college classes. A fellow named Bill, the only one owning a car, was driving back to Chicago. He offered to take me and another boy, Don Creekbaum, to share in driving and expense. Each of us paid him $10. Don and I were less experienced drivers than Bill, so I felt a little uneasy when Don was driving. At night, when Bill would be sleeping in the back seat, I preferred to stay awake and help watch the road. The roads and highways were all two lane, which meant we were frequently meeting oncoming traffic. Many of the roads were narrow and not altogether safe.

Late one night I noticed our car was crossing the center line heading toward an oncoming truck! Glancing over at Creekbaum I noticed that he was asleep at the wheel! Immediately, I reached across, grabbed the steering wheel and jerked the car back into our lane, barely missing the truck as it sailed past with the horn blaring!

Creekbaum snapped awake when I grabbed the wheel out of his hands, just in time to catch a terrifying glimpse of the truck careening past us as his blaring horn faded in the distance. If I had been sleeping, none of us would have lived to tell the story. I am thankful for God's protection over me in narrow escapes like that one.

When we reached Chicago, Bill took me out to the edge of town, which was a good place to catch a ride. There I began my trek of hitchhiking down Highway 41, the final leg to reach home. It was a happy reunion being with all my family again. Because I made good time getting home, there were a few days remaining before returning to school. It was easy to fall right in with Pop and my brothers doing the usual farm work and chores, until it was necessary to take my leave to return to Purdue.

Meanwhile, outside the sphere of my personal life, the war was intensifying. Even before I left for Montana, news had come of a serious air and sea battle at the tiny Midway Island in the Pacific some 1,300 miles from Hawaii. At a later time, more was learned of the American and Japanese strategies regarding the maneuvers and how they led to the eventual outcome of the battle. The United States maintained some military installations and landed airplanes on Midway Island. The Japanese realized it was a strategic location and an asset to the Americans. They also knew that particular island could be useful to them in their plans to continue their expansion to other islands of the Pacific.

Just six months after the attack on Pearl Harbor, Japan planned to invade Midway Island. In early June of 1942, a flotilla of four carriers (four of the six carriers that took part in the Pearl Harbor attack) carrying 248 planes, 2 battleships, and 15 support ships were headed toward Midway for an invasion of the island. It was to be a surprise attack on June 4. That would lure the American ships to the defense and the Japanese would be prepared to attack with their planes loaded with torpedoes and bombs. One report stated that 4,500 troops and massive supplies were on the American support ships heading to the island.

What the Japanese did not know was that American code breakers knew of their plans; how many ships there were, their approach to the island, and just where they would be. The *surprise* would be on the Japanese, because the Americans set up an ambush. There would be three aircraft carriers with 233 fighter planes, and twenty-five support ships to meet them at just the right time. The three-day battle brought heavy losses to the Japanese.

The decisive defeat of the Japanese was devastating to their navy. All 248 planes were destroyed, one heavy cruiser lost, all four carriers sunk, and 3,057 killed. One U.S. carrier, the *Yorktown,* was sunk. We also lost one destroyer, 150 aircraft and 307 men were killed. [United States Military Archives and Wikipedia, the Free Encyclopedia]

Juggling School and World Events

My income from the forestry job had placed me in a good financial position. It was sufficient to pay for my next semester school tuition with quite a bit of money left over for clothing and other school needs. While I was home attending the Petersburg Church of God, I learned that Roy Cline (a man who was friendly to our church), had a small house trailer that he was selling for $150. I bought the trailer thinking it would provide a better living arrangement for me. I could be free from having to work for my rent and it would give me more uninterrupted time to study. It would also be nice not having to be housed in with noisy students.

After buying the trailer I still had enough of my summer earnings left for school startup needs. I made a trip to Lafayette in our family's 1934 Plymouth to register for classes and look for a place to park the trailer. I also inquired about my job at the meat locker plant. Tom Gould, the owner, was glad to have me return and even gave me a five-cent raise, which would be 30 cents per hour.

Upon my return home, Imel (my eldest brother) pulled the trailer to Lafayette for me with his 1935 pickup truck. My younger brothers, Morris and Orace Wayne, as well as Eugene Willis (a friend from school) went along to help set the trailer, while also having a little adventure. I took my old bicycle along to use for transportation, because my trailer was going to be about a half mile from campus. My bicycle was an old 28-inch *clincher wheel*, which was a good riding bike.

The house trailer made living at Purdue quite different. It was an easy half mile ride on my bike to and from my destinations on campus and to work at the meat locker. I arrived home each evening, or whenever there was time during the day, to a quiet place for study and to prepare my own meals. The trailer had an electric stove for cooking, which provided the means to prepare the special cuts of meat Mr. Gould sometimes gave to me.

Most of my day was spent on campus at the library, when not in class. That put me closer to the locker plant when it was time to report for evening work. During the winter days, I could turn on the electric heater when I arrived at the trailer. It didn't take long before it would be cozy and warm. That was much more agreeable than contending with the late night confusion and noise from the other fellows in the apartment the previous year.

By the end of that fall semester, the war department was continuing to draft 18-year-olds into the army. I knew that it was about my turn to be drafted into the military. I did not want to pay the next semester's tuition, then be drafted and lose the money that I had paid. College students were being deferred for the time being, but I did not know how long that would prevail. Therefore, at the end of the first semester, I used my folks' 1934 Plymouth to pull my trailer back home and sold it for almost the amount that I had paid for it. I decided to help Imel with the farm work and assist around home until I would be drafted, which was almost a certainty.

CHAPTER THREE

UNCLE SAM, MY SCHOOLMASTER
Camp Atterbury

![Pike County Courthouse, Petersburg, Indiana]

Pike County Courthouse, Petersburg, Indiana

On the morning of September 14, 1944, a big Greyhound bus rolled to a stop in front of the Pike County Courthouse in Petersburg. It was there to pick up several of us who had "won" a free U.S. Army induction trip. The night before my departure on that unknown journey was a restless one. The morning arrived for me to leave home, having an uncertain future before me. I heard Mom moving about in the kitchen, which was a common sound each morning. She was up earlier than usual, no doubt she hadn't slept well either. As the day had drawn nearer, signs of worry could be detected in her actions and expression. Still, she had tried to be strong and encouraging, as was her way. While I was getting myself dressed, she was not only preparing the usual big breakfast for the family, she was also making sure I had a good lunch packed for my journey. There was such love in our home and I especially felt it then. Mom handed me the lunch that she lovingly prepared for my travels. As the tears welled up in her eyes, Mom gave me one last big hug, making it difficult to leave. With an ache in our hearts we all said our *goodbyes*, then Imel drove me to town and stayed until my bus pulled out.

The bus had come from the neighboring city of Princeton and was already half full of men who had also received their draft notices. A total of 40 young men were then on the bus headed to Camp Atterbury, which was a military camp near Columbus, Indiana. Some of those who got on with me in Petersburg were acquaintances: George Schmidt, James Johns, Jessie Quiggins, and Melvin Willis (my cousin), then there was Jack Bishop and Robert Parks from Princeton. Some others were familiar, but not enough to know them by name. Seeing the faces of people I knew, also being inducted, relieved some of the apprehension of the unknown.

Dewey Hawes, a Boy Scout leader from our community, was there to see us off, as was his custom each time a group of fellows left for the military. He shook hands with each one, including me. He also gave me a new scout pocketknife as a going away present. It was a treasured gift that was put to good use as well as a fond reminder of my hometown folks.

The ride to Camp Atterbury that day would have been much more pleasant if there had been less alcohol aboard the bus. Some of the guys had brought their bottle of *spirits* along, as if that was the last drinking opportunity of their life. In addition to the drinking, many of them were using very foul language. It was almost as if they were trying to see who could be the most offensive. Not being accustomed to hearing such vile talk, it was very abrasive. The more intoxicated they got, the louder and more raucous the revelry became. What could have been a pleasurable adventure became more of a nauseating endurance. The bus driver had to stop twice for some of them to vomit and use "the bathroom of the great outdoors". When we arrived at Atterbury, James Johns and Jessie Quiggens were still so drunk, the military police immediately took them to sober up in the camp jail. I never did see them again. Later, Melvin learned that one of them had slipped off and went home! The rest of us were taken to some barracks, where we were assigned a sleeping cot. Soon thereafter we were lined up to go for supper in the mess hall where, to my amazement, they were feeding over 2,000 men! I was awestruck by the enormity of that huge dining hall–I had never seen anything like it in my life.

Being processed at Camp Atterbury took about four days. Early the first morning everyone was called out to go pick up his issue of army duds. It seemed odd that some things fit and some didn't. We had to take what was given to us regardless of how it fit. Next we were lined up at a dispensary and given several shots of vaccines. I was assigned KP duty at the mess hall, where four of us were given the job of peeling potatoes all day. We peeled and peeled and peeled...potato after potato! In that one day we peeled so many potatoes, we thought we never wanted to see another potato again!

Those of us who had been there a few days started becoming aware of the many new arrivals. Some of the newcomers had the dazed look of a person who is trying to wake from a bad dream. Many others had the appearance that comes with the realization that they have just stepped into a seriously threatening situation. The new guys still wore their civilian clothes, while we "old-timers" were correctly dressed as real soldiers.

One evening while we were waiting, four abreast in line for dinner, we saw a young man walking toward us. It was obvious he had just arrived as he was all decked out in a fancy suit. Not just a regular suit either, it was one of an extraordinarily loud style called the *zoot suit*, popular at that time. That style of suit had a jacket that was heavily padded with broad square shoulders, extremely wide lapels, and extended down nearly to the knees. The pleated pants were brightly colored and worn with broad suspenders matching the large fancy bow tie. Whoever he was, he presented such an odd sight among a sea of army uniforms. As the man strutted down the street, his suit shimmered in the sun and his brightly colored tie flashed in contrast. He was like a walking target for men eager to ridicule. George Schmidt, always the comedian, yelled out loud enough to be heard, "Well, look what's a'comin' down the street!" That raised a lot of laughter from the men accustomed to razzing each other.

Early one morning the order was given for us to all get packed and dressed in our khaki uniforms, ready to be shipped out, *on the double*! (Everything was done *on the double*.) We paraded to a railroad station where we loaded onto a troop train. It was several cars long and pulled by a big steam locomotive.

I liked being on a train again. The whistle blew frequently as we traveled through the night. The sound brought memories of the many night-time trains passing our house, situated very near a railroad. I even enjoyed the novelty of the simple meals served to us in our personal mess gear. According to the direction of the sun and the names of stations we passed, I could determine that we were going in a southerly direction. It seemed peculiar to me that our destination was not revealed to us. I was to learn later, it was standard practice with the military not to discuss with troops their destination. That may be a part of where we derived the common term of something being *a military secret*. In practicality, it was unnecessary for us to know anything other than that we were going somewhere for basic training. After all, we had no choice in the matter! It also prepared us not to expect to know a lot of war details, when we were later moved from place to place.

There was some concern among the men just to learn that we were headed for *undergoing* basic training. There was no shortage of rumors, speaking of that as being a really rough ordeal. Although it wasn't something I was particularly looking forward to, I just thought that if others can accomplish it I will make the best of it too.

A few stops were made along the way, the train jolted us each time. It was something else to wonder about among ourselves. The train was not picking up other passengers at any of the stations, so why the stops? We did not feel questions would be welcomed. Finally, the train came to a stop among several buildings with army vehicles sitting around. This gave us the assumption we had reached some kind of army base and it surely must be our destination.

Even though it was an army base, the area was quite attractive with all the nearby pine trees and other unusual vegetation. A sergeant came aboard the train and began barking out some orders. He did so in such a fast, forceful way that no one could understand his words, but it did seem to convey...*get off the train*! We soon learned his harsh manner was the typical way most commands were delivered. His unfriendly welcome underscored the rumors, of basic training being rough, as true. He certainly confirmed it to us! So with renewed realization of trouble ahead, we filed off the train and lined up as had been the practice at Camp Atterbury.

Basic Training at Camp Blanding

Once we all were unloaded and standing in place, the sergeant began giving marching orders in a strange unintelligible language. I could tell that most guys in our group knew nothing about marching, but they did understand just enough of his intentions to get moving in the right direction. Like a herd of sheep we managed to get in line and follow him to a staging area. My ROTC training at Purdue helped me to know the meaning of his orders and the others quickly learned in the space of a very few days. Even though his dramatics were a comical sight, the sergeant left us in no doubt what our business was and that he was quite serious about our doing it.

The sergeant took us to a staging area for a short period of orientation by a captain and a lieutenant. The orientation was partially a repeat of lectures we had already heard at Camp Atterbury, along with some added information about our new assignment and what we would be doing. We were told of some strict rules to follow: dress code, conduct, procedure in the dining hall, our hours of training, and so forth. Among other pertinent information, they further explained that we were in Camp Blanding, Florida, and would be there for a 17-week training program. Florida seemed to be an ideal place for a training camp because we did not have to contend with extremely cold weather.

Finally, three sergeants began calling out names, dividing us into separate groups. The *companies* were lined up and taken in different directions to places where there were groups of little buildings called *huts*. The huts were bare, which had only five cots arranged around the walls (two along the sides and one at the end opposite the door) and we each had a footlocker. That constituted all of our furnishings. Hut assignments were made according to alphabet. The men in my hut were Wheeler, Willis, Wright, Young, and Zeller. In the army everyone was called by their last name. I never learned their first names, except on the few occasions when I became better friends with someone. Our sergeant came to each hut and gave some housekeeping rules. Everything had to be done according to regulation. Foot lockers, shelves, bed covers, clothing and everything had to be in a certain place, arranged a certain way. Inspections would be made frequently and any violation could result in KP duty or some even more unpleasant task. Most of the guys in B Company, to which I was assigned, had some college or other type of training. That proved to be the reason we were together; assigned to what was designated as a Combat Engineer Company. That meant we had to take all of the basic infantry training. Additionally, we received courses in methods of improvised construction that could be applied in combat situations.

James Willis and friend, Bill Wheeler (R)
by their hut at Camp Blanding, Florida

At first we *new recruits* got plenty of marching and physical exercise, but otherwise basic training was not proving to be very rigorous or punishing.

Everywhere we went for a day of training we marched to cadence (one, two, one, two...). One of the lieutenants, who sometimes accompanied our marching, would make it a little humorous by calling, "You had a good home and you LEFT, RIGHT, LEFT, your grandma was RIGHT, LEFT, RIGHT..." repeating the same thing over and over at different intervals. The M-1 rifle was always on our shoulder every day, wherever we went. At the end of our march, no matter where it was, we *stacked arms* (leaning them together in groups of three) ready to pick up again when moving on. The rifles had a unique mark on each one, so we always knew how to recognize our own.

Sometimes, much of our day would be spent in lecture. We marched to the training area, stacked arms, then sat on bleachers for lectures about war strategy, nomenclature of equipment, and other such things. The lieutenant often added a little humor to keep our attention and interest. At other times our activities would be a little rugged. One day they marched us to an area where there was a section of rope ladders 20 feet high. The section was wide enough that six guys could climb at a time. The object was to climb up, go over the pole at the top, and climb down the other side. That was a fun exercise for most of us. A few found it to be a struggle both ways. Every trainee had to go over the top of the rope ladder five times. I wondered how climbing a ladder had anything to do with fighting a war. I was to find out!

For everyday regular training we wore a fatigue shirt and trousers. One day, after having been there a few weeks and having learned to march in good formation, we were ordered to don our dress uniforms. Some general or other dignitary was coming to the base. There would be a dress parade for his reception and inspection on the parade ground. Several times, for a few weeks, the sergeant had spent some time teaching us to march formally, four abreast. He was very strict about keeping those lines straight in all directions and keeping in step without fail. His voice was very loud and firm. There was no doubt in anyone's mind that he meant business! The whole performance of the several companies lasted at least two hours. We actually didn't mind showing off a little, but there was one period of 20 minutes in which we were required to stand at attention the entire time. Twenty minutes with no moving and without an end in sight, was extremely wearing. We thought we might hear a word or two of praise for our efforts, but it was not to be. We got no report at all regarding it, either complimentary or critical. Our reward was a good lunch in the mess hall after changing into fatigue clothes.

Many of the trainees complained about the food. However, we got three meals each day, always served on time. I thought they were usually good and well prepared. Sometimes for breakfast, the kitchen sergeant served fried eggs, allowing each fellow to say how he wanted the eggs prepared. The sergeant would then throw the eggs on a plate for the fellow.

Personally, I thought the guys had no room for complaint. It was always a welcome treat to come back to a hot meal each evening after being out with only field rations for lunch. Sometimes the kitchen staff would bring a hot lunch to the area where we were.

An Unexpected Encounter

On the first Sunday at Camp Blanding, an announcement was made inviting fellows in our platoon to the chapel for church service. A sergeant would escort any of us to church who wanted to go. The information was that we were to be properly dressed, in khaki uniform with a necktie, and be ready at 9:30 am on Sunday morning. The trip would be made marching, as usual, in formation. Once there, we would be expected to sit in a group, as designated by the sergeant. The reason for the escort was that we were not permitted out of our living area for the first two weeks without an escort. Only 12 guys from our whole platoon of 60 chose to attend. We quietly filed in and were seated in two rows of pews near the back of a pleasant chapel. The soft organ music set a respectful atmosphere for the service, which was soon to start. Being there gave me a good feeling, and I anticipated a meaningful worship service.

Before many people arrived, I noticed a white haired soldier sitting near the front of the sanctuary, who had a familiar look to him. Studying him from my vantage point, I tried to place him. Then I recognized that he was Ralph Onyet, a young man from Petersburg, whose father was the local blacksmith. Ralph had been in my high school class! Ralph and I had even taken many of the same classes throughout our four years at PHS. Although it was temporarily violating our seating arrangement, I risked a disciplinary assignment and made my way up front to greet him. Seated beside him was a young lady who was evidently his wife. To my astonishment, I knew her immediately!

She was the former Hilda Mae Willis! When we were youngsters, we had been elementary classmates at Willis School near Clark's Station. At that time I thought she was my girlfriend because she acted like she liked me, but I was always too timid to tell her I liked her. What a surprise to see Hilda Mae there and to learn that Ralph had married her. I was glad for them and wished God's blessings on them to have a happy married life. I had no desire to be a married man while in the military service. Although, the thought crossed my mind, "The Lord will have a good and lovely young lady, somewhere waiting, just for me when I get out of the service."

In that brief visit, I learned Ralph had been in the army for about two years. He was not in the infantry training as I was. Rather, he was in a support service there at the camp. Ralph and Hilda had an apartment off base for the time he would be serving at that assignment. They in turn learned I was a "rookie", a newcomer to the base.

The church service did not disappoint me. It was very beautiful and reverently conducted, if quite formal. It was not the more relaxed type of worship service I was accustomed to. Nevertheless, I continued attending the chapel almost every Sunday while in training at Camp Blanding. Regardless of the type of service, wherever I can attend church, I always look to the Lord in prayer and worship in my own way.

I watched for my friends, Ralph and Hilda, on subsequent Sundays but I did not see them again. Later I learned that he had been transferred to another military base. What a remarkable coincidence that we met there in the army chapel, 900 miles from our southern Indiana homes, on their last Sunday to attend.

Maggie's Drawers!

We had been carrying our rifles day after day, and understood their importance, but we knew little about that particular one and had not yet used any ammunition in it. One day the lieutenant told us we would go to a building set up for instruction in nomenclature of the M-1 rifle. I hardly knew what the word meant, but assumed it meant to learn details about the function of our gun. The instructing officer first taught us the relatively easy procedure of how to disassemble the rifle into four main parts: the trigger assembly, the stock, the firing mechanism, and the barrel.

That part was simple and we all had fun playing with those pieces. The M-1 was designed to be quickly broken down for cleaning and reassembly. Next, was the more difficult task of taking the trigger assembly completely apart and correctly putting it back together. We had to learn to disassemble the many little springs, pins, levers and various other parts. It was not simple to do, but the instructor was very thorough in the explanation of the process. It wasn't long until I could take it apart and get it back together rather quickly. Rifles were not completely foreign to me. Putting that "puzzle" together was interesting and a lot of fun. Some of the guys had real difficulty with that job, never having had experience with guns. We were expected to accomplish and repeat that process in a limited time frame.

In the evenings, while resting in our huts, we were expected to practice taking the M-1 apart and putting it back together. Zeller, one of the five in our hut, refused to practice taking the trigger assembly apart because it was just too difficult to put back together. One evening, while he was gone to the PX for a snack, I decided to play a trick on him and at the same time force the issue of his learning that needed skill. I swiftly disassembled his rifle and trigger assembly. Then folding back the covers on his cot, I placed all 40 some parts between his sheets. When Zeller returned, to his dismay, he found his rifle was missing from the spot where he had left it. He was furious because he knew we were supposed to guard our rifles with our lives! None of us would tell him where to find it, but when he sat on his bunk, realization dawned. Under his bed covers Zeller found the mixed up pile of pieces that had been his rifle. He was sure I had done it and accused me of the prank. He was faced with an enormous problem! It had to be ready the next day. He was extremely upset and frustrated because he knew there was no possible way he would be able to put it back together by himself. We watched his reaction with interest and some amusement, but when I saw that he was distraught almost to tears, I felt sorry for him. At that point I put his rifle back together for him. Perhaps his relief that I reassembled it, kept him from holding the prank against me.

After carrying the M-1 rifle every day, with it empty of any live ammunition, there came the day we were taken to the rifle range. On that day we used live ammunition for the first time. Practicing at the rifle range was interesting, even if the thought of using that rifle to shoot a person was unsettling to my nature. The handling of guns was a familiar experience to me because we used guns to provide food for the table at home. Each of us was given a few practice shots and taught how to *zero* our rifles, also known as *training the sights* on a target. Then we were put to the test to see how well we could hit the target. We spent several hours on the rifle range shooting at targets from different distances. One of the targets was a large white sign with circles and a bull's eye in the middle. A worker in the pit would withdraw the target each time a shot was fired and report the score back to the officer on the firing line who kept score. If the shot missed the target completely, the pit guy would wave a flag on a pole in the air and everyone would yell, "Maggie's Drawers!" Each soldier would receive an average of all his scores to determine if he earned an expert, sharpshooter, marksman, or failure badge. I hit the bull's eye every time, except for one shot that hit the target in an outer ring. I earned the Expert Rifleman Badge. At the same time, I avoided the yelling of Maggie's Drawers at me! Curiously, even if a soldier failed the rifle range test, he was still qualified to carry a rifle and remain in the infantry! But perhaps not so curious, for if failing the test kept one out of the infantry then the number of poor shots might have risen dramatically.

Nine pits were stationed at different distances on a separate firing range; number one rather close with each subsequent pit a little farther, number nine being 100 yards distant. Each pit contained a soldier holding up a target which was shaped like the upper torso of a human body. I found it distinctly unpleasant shooting at something that looked like a person, but I had no choice. If a shot hit the target the pit guy lowered the target. When it came my turn, I hit every target except the last one. Being a country boy, with a dad who made sure I could bring home a rabbit for dinner, was making me look real good! We practiced on the rifle range for two days.

Periodically, all guns were emptied of ammunition and stacked properly while shooters exchanged places with pit workers. I had a turn in one of the round target pits and had to wave the flag occasionally. Some of the guys had a hard time with the rifle target practice.

PVT James Willis holding his M-1 rifle, which was carried all through training. Photo taken in front of his hut at Camp Blanding, Florida.

The M-1 rifle was the main weapon used by all infantrymen in the U.S. Army during World War II, but we were trained in the usage and operation of various other types of weapons. We also spent a day at a different shooting range, where we fired a bazooka a few times. It was the most difficult to use. The bazooka was for shooting grenades, as opposed to tossing them. They were so impractical to carry around and awkward to use that they were not used in combat to any extent. In addition to the bazooka, we practiced with a device mounted onto the M-1 that made it capable of launching grenades. It had a fierce kick to it, whereas the bazooka had very little kick at all. It seemed to me, learning the use of those two weapons was a waste of time and effort.

We also practiced with machine guns. Working in teams of two we learned how to load and feed rounds of ammunition, as well as firing at a target. Each pair took turns firing the weapon to ensure that every soldier would be capable of using the machine gun, if called upon. Our target for those exercises was a remote operated drone; a scaled down model airplane. The machine guns were highly effective and used very extensively.

Much of the basic training was neither difficult nor undesirable. Even KP duty, in which every soldier was eventually required to participate, wasn't too bad. However, there were three particular details which I could not appreciate.

Every night six soldiers from each unit were assigned to walk guard duty. Two different assigned areas were patrolled by two of the soldiers for two hours. At the end of that time, the sergeant of the guard would bring two others to relieve them. The cycle was repeated through the night, whereby each of us assigned to guard duty were on two hours and off four hours.

The instructions for the person on guard duty included walking with rifle at *port-arms*. That meant on his shoulder, ready to draw if necessary. The rifle was unloaded but we were to pretend that it was loaded. If we met a stranger in the area while on duty, we were to challenge them and ask for their rank and serial number or other identification. I always wondered about that! What would I do if the person refused or ran away? However, I never had to challenge anyone! Guarding that area, without bullets, indicated to me that there was no real threat. Perhaps it was more of a preparatory exercise for when it would be truly critical.

Another less desirable job was when all men were lined up at the edge of the camp and asked to go through the camp and "police the area". That amounted to picking up anything that did not grow. There were cigarette stubs in several places, because most of the guys were smokers in those days. I had never smoked in my life, therefore picking up cigarette butts was repulsive. So much so that I would pretend not to see the stubs and leave them for a smoker to retrieve.

For me, the most undesirable part of all the training at Camp Blanding was bayonet practice. Each rifle carried a bayonet on the underneath side of the barrel. After marching to a certain area, the order was given to "fix bayonets." That meant detaching the bayonet from the underneath side of the rifle and affixing onto the proper place at the end of the barrel.

Some dummies were hung for us to practice stabbing. I could hardly bear the very thought of sticking a bayonet through anyone. That was surely a most horrible method of warfare! There had been news and information of situations already in this war, where the infantrymen had gotten involved in hand-to-hand combat. I fervently prayed to God that I would never come to that sort of situation. If I did, the army maintained very strict discipline and no one ever disobeyed a command from an officer.

Frequently, the officers spoke to us regarding the war our country was fighting in Europe and in the Pacific. They impressed upon us that we were being trained as replacements to assist in the war effort. However, they refrained from going into too many details. We seldom heard about the severity of the situation in any of the war areas, perhaps for a purpose. Neither did the officers ever give us any indication as to whether we would be going East or West at the end of our training.

One guy in our company, Homer Billings, became a closer friend than any of the others. It seemed an unlikely friendship at the time, because he was a Catholic and I was a Protestant. But what we did have in common was that we both held firmly to our Christian beliefs and standards. He was in a different platoon, but we enjoyed chumming together. In the evenings, often we would walk to the PX for refreshments. Regardless of religious persuasion, a close bond developed between all of us in the platoon because of enduring all the rigors of basic training together.

During the four months at Camp Blanding I did not know of any dispute, fight, or serious argument between any of the guys. The only complaint I heard was about the food. An outing sometimes provided a diversion for any who chose to participate. Most of the time the excursions were not of interest to me. However, one was an offer of a free army bus ride to Silver Springs Outdoor Nature Park at Ocala, Florida. Homer and I decided to sign up for it. The well-manicured park was lush with a brilliant array of colorful flowers and other attractive plants. The park service offered us free rides on their glass bottom boats from which we could observe marine life. In addition to a variety of sea animals and vegetation, we could see fish investigating a wrecked vessel beneath the surface of the water. That Saturday excursion was a pleasant escape from our more serious business.

During the 14th week, our platoon was to build a makeshift bridge across a ravine. An army truck took us a few miles from camp to a wooded area, where there was an abundance of small trees. We were set to cutting specified size trees that would supply the posts and poles needed for constructing the bridge. Sometimes, there were so many of us working on the same thing that we actually got in the way of one another. Within three days we completed a 20-foot bridge, stable enough to carry a medium sized truck. That task was considered the combat engineering part of our training.

Bivouac with Blistered Buddies

During the final two weeks of Boot Camp, the entire company went on a simulated combat training exercise called a *bivouac*. That included a 20-mile march carrying a full battle pack weighing 50 pounds, in addition to our rifle. We were advised to change our socks at every break, which was each hour of the march. I appreciated that advice and changed my socks when we stopped for a rest. By the time we stopped, my feet would be hot and sweaty. Some of the guys did not heed the advice and ended up with blisters. A few were in such pain that they could not make it the full distance and were picked up by the army truck, following along behind us. We had done a lot of practice marching up to that point, but were still not prepared for a march of such length. Marching 20 miles was truly a test of endurance. I was glad to pass the test. That is, I made it to the end under my own power and did not have to be picked up by the truck.

Neither did I develop any blisters on my feet. Through such exercises we became stronger by becoming more fully aware of our own strengths and weaknesses. We also learned that sometimes there were reasons for certain instructions, even when it made no sense to us.

Those two weeks were spent simulating some very real combat situations. On one obstacle course, we had to crawl on our bellies for about 30 yards beneath an entanglement of barbed wire with machine guns periodically firing overhead. We were also assigned to do some scouting at night with a compass and flashlight. Two days we spent divided up into two combat teams, firing at the opposing team with blank shells in the rifles. We were given a stern warning not to fire the rifle too close to our pretended enemy, because some fire would shoot out even with blanks.

Since we were camping out, sleeping in pup tents, a field kitchen prepared most of our meals. On days in which our military exercises took us too far afield from the kitchen, we were initiated to field rations. At the end of the two weeks the field kitchen prepared a sack lunch, for us to carry in our packs, for the return trip to Camp Blanding.

When those training exercises concluded, we would soon bid farewell to all our buddies, with whom we had become acquainted. A few more days were spent in lectures about destinations, along with words of encouragement. Some more marching was done, as well as being assigned to menial tasks, and we were sent to the lecture rooms for further preparation as to what we might expect.

Each man was given shipping orders, a 20-day furlough, and vouchers to cover their travel expense. My orders were to report to Fort Ord, California, just north of San Francisco. I knew then I would definitely be going to the Pacific War Theater.

The furlough was a real blessing. I had written ahead, before leaving Florida, making a special request of my dad. He was always known as an honest and honorable man, a good provider and a hard worker. That is the legacy he left to all of his children. But when he became involved in politics, he had taken up the bad habit of drinking alcohol. On some weekends he would come home in an unstable condition after he had been on a drinking binge. I did not want to see him like that during the precious few days I would have with him. Hoping to prevent it, I wrote this letter:

Dear Pop,

I will be home for a short 20-day visit in a few days. Then, I will be leaving for some unknown destination in this awful war, for which I have been training. We all know that I will likely be in a position of serious danger, and that many soldiers do not return. I have faith in God that I will not be one of them, but I am prepared to let it be according to His will. Let me make a special request! Please do not drink any alcohol while I'm at home this time. This will be the last time I see you before going to war, and I want to see you sober as my honorable and respectable father. Respectfully, from your son, James

PFC James B. Willis

Furlough and Farewell to Friends

During my furlough Pop did honor my request. I don't know if he ever started back to drinking. I do not recall seeing him in that condition any time after that. He was in a cheerful mood and expressed interest in my situation. Pop was working at a factory in Washington, Indiana, called Corcoran's, and was only home evenings and weekends. Other family members were also at work most of the days I was there. Things at home and the surrounding community appeared just the same as when I left four months ago. It was winter time with no opportunity to help with outside chores. The animals had been sold, but Mom still had a good flock of chickens.

While there I took advantage of every opportunity to attend church in Petersburg. It was so restorative to be back among the faithful; worshipping in the comfort and familiarity of my home church. It was very different from the stiff, formal military church services. The pleasant wholesomeness of the services and the joy of seeing Christian friends were immensely uplifting. Friends and relatives were glad to see me, greeting me with smiles, hugs, and handshakes. Often they wanted to talk about the war, which was on everyone's mind. Some wanted to commiserate with me by offering their well-meant sympathy that I had to go. Their words of pity and worry were distinctly uncomfortable. Well wishes, promises to write and pray for me would have been more welcome.

It was an adventure, as well as a duty for me, therefore I did not want sympathy; neither did I want to be considered a hero. Boys all across the nation were serving as I was.

I felt my destiny was in the hands of God, as I recalled a verse from the 23rd Psalm: "Yea, though I walk through the valley of the shadow of death, I shall fear no evil, for thou art with me. Thy rod and Thy staff they comfort me."

CHAPTER FOUR

THE PACIFIC THEATER

From Fort Ord to Hawaii

My furlough was over much too quickly before it came time to say goodbye again. My brother, Imel, took me to Princeton where I boarded a train for Chicago. Ever since the Midwest was settled, Chicago has been a major hub for commerce and travel. The evidence of that was clear as my train pulled into the Chicago station. There were trains everywhere, more than I had ever seen in one place and the huge station was crowded with military guys going in all directions. It was a mass of confusion to me. I began to wonder if I would find my way out of that place.

I looked around for a place to ask questions or someone who might direct me, but it seemed that everyone had their own concerns and no time to assist strangers. Finally, with the help of some attendants, the train I was to board was located and my gear was loaded. The train was crowded with soldiers, many of them going to Fort Ord in California, just like me. It was always easy to make friends with other soldiers, even complete strangers, because we were all there for a common cause.

I found my seat and exchanged greetings with the guys around me.

I had been to St. Louis and to Montana. Now I was given a chance to see more of the vast farm lands and mountains of the American landscape. It was pleasant just to sit there, relaxing, looking at all the different sights. On that three-day trip across the United States, I was seeing places and things of which I had only heard about. It caused me to consider the difficulties of the brave pioneers, enduring many hardships, as they traveled those many miles with a slow moving wagon train.

We had all been given vouchers for meals on the train. At the end of the train ride, hundreds of us were transferred to a large ferry to cross the bay. From there, we were bussed to Fort Ord.

Fort Ord

During the few days at Fort Ord, we were processed and organized for a trip to Seattle, Washington. Another soldier and I caught a bus to go sightseeing in downtown San Francisco. While there, I found and bought an expensive shockproof Swiss watch that cost me $60. That was a lot of money in a time when the average wage was about $6 a day. However, I was not going to need that money where I was going. I wanted to have a good waterproof watch, because we had heard that we might be in jungles and in places where it would be best to have one that was waterproof and shockproof.

It gave me special satisfaction to own a good watch. It became even more meaningful as I carried it through my military years and for a few years afterward.

As we were being called out and preparing to board a troop train to Seattle, a captain in charge asked for six volunteers for KP duty during the trip. That meant three days of working in the train's kitchen car. My hand shot up quickly for that job! He finally got five more volunteers. Not only did I find it interesting to see how things were handled in a train car kitchen, the job was also fun. We were given special bunks in the coach next to the kitchen car, but we did not spend much time in our bunks. It was more interesting to sit in the open boxcar and watch the wonderful mountain scenery we were passing through. That was our entertainment and pastime when we were not working.

One of the things I liked best on that job was serving meals. The meals were served one car at a time. All of the guys in one car would come through with their mess gear to receive their portion of food. That would continue until they all had been served. We tolerated some very unfriendly "compliments", as if it would improve the quality or quantity of food served.

There were about eight coaches in all to be served. When the men finished eating they all had to go back through and wash their mess gear in large tubs of water. Our job was to occasionally change the water.

Again we heard a barrage of griping along with some foul words, as a reward for our outstanding dining service.

The cook would only smile with us and say, "You are not at Grandma's kitchen now!"

All of us workers in the kitchen would just smile and enjoy the complaints. We were not about to get fired from our special jobs. We could enjoy our meal of good helpings, sitting in the box car with the big door open, watching the scenery as we traveled. When back in my bunk at night, I would read some from my New Testament that I carried with me to keep in touch with the Lord.

It was night when our train pulled into Seattle. We were loaded onto a convoy of 10 army trucks waiting to take us to a base about 30 minutes away. Security was so tight in Seattle that we were restricted to the base. We were not allowed to go out for the purpose of exploring the area and seeing the sights. For security reasons, there was obscurity surrounding the precise location of our camp. I learned later that we were at Fort Lawton, which was in the northwest corner of the county near Puget Sound.

During the war, Seattle was considered a prime target for Japanese attacks because it was a significant industrial center on the west coast, and perhaps more importantly, it was home of Boeing. Thousands of Boeing airplanes were built in Seattle during the war. Seattle was also a major seaport and deep in Puget Sound was the Bremerton Naval Ship yards where U.S. warships were repaired and prepared for battle.

Seattle was considered a potential *hotbed* for espionage activities, not only because of Boeing and the shipyards, but also because of the large population of Japanese people who had settled there. It was feared that there might be some Japanese sympathizers among them. In an agonizing but necessary decision, President Roosevelt ordered all persons of Japanese descent, even if they were U.S. citizens, move to detention camps for their own safety as well as for the security of the production facilities in the region.

The huge Boeing airplane factory had imitation houses built on top of the building, so that any spy or other observer from the air could not see the plant. It looked just like a residential area without any hint of a factory beneath it.

Water, Water, Everywhere

We were at Fort Lawton four rainy days. Then late one night they took a large group of us to board a troop ship. Later that same night, the ship moved out of the harbor to minimize detection. For military security, standard practice was to make large troop movements late at night, presumably when the spies were more likely to be sleeping or could not easily take pictures! The dock that night was a busy place, with trucks coming and going, delivering supplies and soldiers.

[A.E. Willis illustration]

Huge pallets of food and equipment were being swung onto the ship with cranes as we climbed the steep gangway up the side of the ship in single file.

At the top was the quarterdeck, where officers with clipboards checked off names and directed us to our quarters below deck. Special precautions were given to watch our heads and lift our feet when stepping through hatches. Even with our helmets on, the low hatches with raised lower edges could deliver a hard knock to the head and entangle the feet. Even with the warning, many soldiers, unaccustomed to the raised hatch edges, found themselves stumbling about in the dimly lit passageways.

Silently, before daylight broke the ship hauled her moorings and slipped away into the harbor. It was smooth sailing for the first part of the day as the ship navigated through the narrow waterway of Puget Sound. The Sound was protected from the large waves of the ocean, so the only motion we felt was when the ship altered speed. That changed quickly when we reached the open sea!

There must have been a storm off the coast of Washington, just waiting for us. The ocean was churning with huge waves and rough winds that caused our ship to pitch and roll. Sometimes the waves would wash completely over the deck. When men went down below for breakfast or lunch, they had to hold their tray or a sudden roll of the ship would slide all trays to one end of the table. Many lost their meal in that way, as no seconds were served. After breakfast the ship was still rolling and rocking, up and down, side to side. Men began to get seasick and were unable to hold down their meal. There were barrels for that purpose around the ship, but some did not make it to the barrel or to the side of the ship in time. The deck got right slippery and smelly, which only added to the misery of tossing in every direction. I was having no trouble with the motion of the ship, even rather enjoyed the rocking and rolling on the waves, until the vile stench hit me. My stomach began to churn because of the smell, so I hurried down below deck to my bunk. There, I could lay on my back and let the rocking of the ship lull me to sleep.

The supper call awakened me and once again I made my way to the dining area. That meal was more civilized than the earlier one had been, as the sea had mercifully calmed down.

Otherwise, time became long on our hands to the point of boredom. Since there was little to do, some of us passed the time at the very front of the ship, watching it repeatedly bob up and down with the waves. Occasionally, the monotony was broken by the amazing sight of flying fish. That was really something to see! I had never known there was such a fish. Astonishingly, they would rise suddenly out of the water and sail above the waves a short distance. Many of the guys passed the time sitting around playing cards and smoking cigarettes. Bringing a book or favorite magazine along never occurred to me, but I occasionally picked up one of the few old magazines lying around.

Two times, during the trip, we were all ordered to go below deck to our bunks. That was when the sailors on board were firing the large guns. As we were given no information as to the reason for this, our imaginations were given free rein. It was an eerie feeling to think they might be defending our ship from an enemy attack. I had heard of the perils of men who go down with a ship. Later, we learned that it was merely a practice session.

Aloha

Five days later, we reached the islands of Hawaii. Thoughts occurred to me how blessed the Pilgrims must have felt to see land, after their sixty-six days on the rough sea. The island of Oahu appeared to be a strange wonderful place! Sadly, also before us was the sobering sight of ships damaged or completely destroyed, still visible where they rested in the harbor. It was to be expected, as it was a result of the bombing of Pearl Harbor some three years earlier, yet the impact of seeing it was staggering.

There lay the USS *Arizona* on its side, on which 1,177 crewmen lost their lives on the fateful day of December 7, 1941. The *Arizona* was the most heavily damaged of all the vessels in Battleship Row, suffering four direct hits. A memorial now exists there to commemorate all the military personnel who lost their lives in the Pearl Harbor attack. Suggestions for a memorial began in 1943. In 1958, President Dwight Eisenhower, who had been instrumental in achieving Allied victory in Europe, approved the creation of the memorial. It was completed in 1961 and dedicated in 1962. As a special tribute to the ship *Arizona* and her lost crew, the United States flag flies from the flagpole still attached to the severed main mast of the sunken battleship.

Upon disembarking, a health checkup was waiting for us and a group of native Hawaiians, who had just returned from the war in Europe. The government did not send Hawaiian soldiers to fight in the war against the Japanese. The physical exam required us all to partially undress. That revealed scars on the Hawaiians, indicating they were war casualties. Seeing all of those fellows carrying the scars of battle was a grim reminder that the war in Germany was still raging and taking lives. Germany had overtaken several European countries, similar to the way Japan was taking over islands of the pacific. Both countries were ruled by dictators, under which many people suffered greatly.

We were glad for the stop on Ohau, Hawaii. Our ultimate destination was not something we looked forward to. So, being in that very different environment gave us something pleasant to think about and do. The island had narrow gauge trains for moving commerce, including small open topped cars for livestock. We were loaded into some of those cattle cars, with standing room only, and taken to a camp back in the hills somewhere. It was rather exciting to ride the little cars and see the beautiful countryside until the engine stopped to take on water. Then it became a problem, as the engine had to build up steam before it could continue up the hill. We had to stand in the hot sun packed in those cars, cramped and crowded, for an hour before moving on. Many of the guys got quite angry, as they became more and more uncomfortable, because of the standing with very little wiggle room. Greatly relieved, we reached our destination and began peeling ourselves loose from the cattle car.

Soon after arriving at camp we had the usual orientation lecture. The officer explained that we would be getting an issue of equipment and clothing, as well as some training for jungle combat. We did not look forward to what that implied. He also recommended we go to town and buy a grass skirt to send home. He explained that the grass skirts were made in Louisiana and sent to Hawaii to sell to soldiers. He told us to go buy one anyway, to make the people back home think the girls there wore grass skirts. I didn't even want to go to town and did not intend to buy a grass skirt. I would not have wanted Pop and Mom to have the grass skirt on display in their store, for customers and friends to see.

At least our camp was actually in a beautiful setting in an undisclosed location, far back in a wooded area of the hills. That made our hikes for training interesting. We also had access to a PX where snacks were available, including 16 oz. cans of pineapple juice for 5 cents. Many of us preferred the pineapple juice to the carbonated drinks.

After a few days of training at our base camp, we marched in a column of two abreast for 10 or 12 miles to a more distant training camp for intense jungle warfare training.

There must have been between two to three hundred soldiers in that march. It seemed like the line stretched out for a half mile or more. We passed by large fields of pineapples, while marching along the road. Some of the guys would drop out of line, run into a field and cut a pineapple with their bayonet. Actually, the officers ought not to have permitted it. My conscience would not allow me to take the pineapples that belonged to the farmers. However, when I saw what looked like a mature pineapple that had been cut, fallen, or thrown into the ditch, I dropped out of line and salvaged that poor pineapple–to the ridicule of other nearby soldiers.

Some said, "Willis, why don't you get you a good one? That one is probably spoiled."

[A.E. Willis Illustration]

When we got to our tents, many of the men were ready to have a party. They began cutting open their pineapples, only to find they were all bitter and green inside because they had not ripened. We had been told that it took 18 months for a pineapple to grow before it was ripe. When I cut mine, it was the only one that was good. I shared it with the others in my tent. Then, they changed their tune. I actually received compliments on the "questionable" pineapple, rather than ridicule!

The jungle training included bayonet practice. We were taught how to affix bayonets to the rifle, in preparation to attack some stuffed dummies "stationed to meet us" as we advanced. After shooting the dummies with blank ammunition, which was simple, we would attack them with our bayonets. I didn't like that exercise and I hoped I would never have to use the bayonet on anyone.

After about a week of jungle warfare training, we marched back to base camp. Upon our arrival to camp, there was nice beautiful Hawaiian music and popular music playing over the loudspeakers. It made for a great welcome back and it boosted our morale.

The next day the cattle cars were awaiting us again. We were herded into them for the return trip to the harbor. Upon our arrival, we could see two troop transport ships waiting for us. As we had grown accustomed to, we were not told where we were being taken. We just followed orders! We did not leave the harbor until both ships were fully loaded. I expect there were as many as a thousand soldiers on each ship that sailed out of the harbor that day.

A Lifetime Friend

Both ships made a stop at the remote little island of Midway, out in the middle of the vast ocean. We did not disembark. The ships sat there in the bay for several hours. No information was given to the troops on board as to the purpose of that stop. Eventually, we moved on out to sea where we were once again surrounded by water, water, and more water.

The waters of the Pacific, in that area, were then practically free of Japanese warships and submarines. That was not the case just two years before when the Japanese were sinking U.S. ships there. Had these waters not been secured, our days would have been spent huddled below deck in general quarters while the ship ran a gauntlet of torpedoes and zeros.

This was our second long trip on the Pacific Ocean. We sailed for six days, but not being told anything made the voyage seem endless. It became somewhat more monotonous than the previous trip, seeing nothing but water everywhere you looked. On the other hand, none of us were in any big hurry because of the suspense (not knowing exactly what we would find at the end of our journey). What lay ahead?

Would it be another stopover, an invasion, or perhaps replacing soldiers already in combat?

WW2- Herbert Wiethorn, son of Henry & Ella Wiethorn

It was on that voyage I met a guy from Texas by the name of Herbert Weithorn. We developed a very close friendship during those few days. Herbert and I were both Christians and had much in common. We had both been reared on a farm and found many things of mutual interest. Neither of us smoked, drank alcohol, or played cards, as was common among the other soldiers. Herbert and I were able to pass the time by finding a magazine to browse or just going to the very front of the ship to watch the waves and talk. We talked about our families, our lives, our backgrounds...sometimes we even talked about what might be in store for us at our next landing. In my private time I continued to pray and trust the Lord that in the end, He would bring me home safely to be with my family.

Weithorn was an early riser, like myself, so we were up in time to see the beautiful sunrise and make the early breakfast call. The ships must have carried loads of food, because we were served good meals the entire way. Sunset was another time that found us at the front of the ship. It appeared that we were sailing right into the stunning red glow of the sun.

Weithorn and I exchanged addresses, so that we could contact each other after the war...if we survived. We made a pact, that we or whichever of us made it home, would contact the other one's family. It was a gruesome thought but, given the times, it was on everyone's mind. We thought our agreement was vital and it gave us a measure of comfort to think that our families would be contacted by someone who knew us.

The Wait before the Storm: Saipan

We finally docked at another island, which we soon learned was called Saipan. Again, it lay somewhere way out in the middle of the great Pacific Ocean. All of these islands were new to most of the guys and the names meant very little other than it was a place to be fighting the Japanese. For the customary security reasons, we were not allowed to off-load from the ship until after dark. Troops disembarked as ordered, but Herbert and I did not leave the ship together. If patterns held true, soldiers were sent out in different groups. Therefore, friends didn't often move off in the same group. Weithorn and I assumed that would be the end of our association together, so we said our *goodbyes*. A convoy of army trucks was waiting to take us to a tent city, where we would be living for the next two or three weeks. We lived with five men in each tent. A large kitchen tent served the hundreds of men with poorly prepared food. It was so inedible that tons of food was just thrown into the garbage.

Saipan was a hilly island, on which the Army engineers had built numerous roads. The U.S. Army also provided a compound for the natives who had survived the war and were displaced from their homes. In fact, I never saw anything that looked like a home until later. There were some places where a few native families put up shacks with whatever materials could be found, but they were not adequate shelters, much less a fit place to live. I understood that the civilian compound was maintained indefinitely with comfortable living quarters and provisions for those who wished to take advantage of it. A separate compound was there for the few Japanese that were taken as prisoners during the battle.

Several weeks prior to our arrival, the U.S. Marines and Infantry had invaded Saipan. The invasion began in the early hours of June 15, 1944, when the U.S. Fifth Fleet, under the leadership of Admiral Spruance, converged on the island. He was known as a smart no-nonsense officer, who had a great dislike for publicity. He had a personal vendetta against Admiral Nagumo, commander of the Japanese Central Pacific Fleet stationed at Saipan. It had been Nagumo who directed the air raids on the U.S. Naval Ships at Pearl Harbor and at Midway. On the day following the raid on Pearl Harbor, Spruance went to the harbor to find the entire U.S Pacific Fleet wiped out and his friends on those ships dead. It was said that he was moved to tears. In his fury and sorrow, he intended to get even in the Battle of Saipan!

At sunrise, the U.S. massive fleet became visible as far as the eye could see. The record showed that Admiral Spruance had amassed 600 ships to wreak vengeance. It was a fleet of 14 battleships, 25 carriers and escorts, 26 cruisers, 144 destroyers, and countless transports. When Admiral Nagumo and his other officers looked through their binoculars, they must have believed American ghosts of Pearl Harbor had returned to haunt them. One might wonder if they then had any regrets of having started the war. It was comparable to the massive 1,600 ships that were gathered for the invasion of Normandy against the Germans in France. Neither the Japanese at Saipan nor the Germans at Normandy could match the American capability of producing massive quantities of materials for such an invasion.

The Japanese officers did not think the American landing-boats, which carried the troops, could reach the shore. They felt safe, but the Seabees had devised an unsinkable steel shell that could clear the reef. The Japanese strategy was to destroy the troops at sea, before they made a landing, or to destroy the landing force at the beachhead. The Japanese high command did not really believe that the U.S. officers would be so bold to invade the Marianas (Saipan, Guam, and Tinian) that were some 1,000 miles from their closest supply base and 3,500 miles from Pearl Harbor. Before the invasion, called *Operation Forager*, Admiral Nagumo admitted that the Marianas were indispensable to the defense of the Japanese homeland.

Bombardment of the island began on June 13, 1944, with 15 battleships firing 165,000 rounds of shells. On the next day, eight other battleships took their place and delivered 2,400 massive 16-inch shells from six miles out in the ocean to soften up the enemy. The Battle of Saipan occurred from June 15 to July 9, 1944. That was during the summer while my deferment was still in place. I was inducted a couple of months later, in September of that year. There were some conflicting reports regarding the numbers of troops on each side and the number of casualties. One reliable source claims the Americans had 71,000 Marines, infantry and support troops. The Japanese had 31,000 men defending the island.

At four o'clock in the morning of June 15, an announcement over the loud speakers, in the crowded quarters below the decks of each landing ship, called for *Battle Stations*. It was the alarm for the imminent battle. Breakfast served in the hot galley would end up being the last meal for some of the marines and infantry.

When news of the invasion reached the Japanese high command in the Philippines, a large Japanese fleet left the Philippines to save Saipan. The fleet was spotted by our submarine, *The Flying Fish*. It was reported that three of the ships were loaded with enemy troops and were headed toward Saipan, possibly for battle replacements. Two of the ships were sunk and the third one disabled. A few of the Japanese soldiers and sailors that had survived the wreckage were rescued from the waters by an American ship and taken as prisoners by the U.S. Navy.

The advance of the Americans was slow and difficult. The island was heavily fortified and the enemy was making use of caves for refuge and firing positions. The rugged terrain also made progress very difficult. There were heavy losses. Finally, by July 7, the Japanese had nowhere to retreat, so they made plans for a suicide attack.

Japanese military, desperate for soldiers, conscripted civilians. Anyone who could walk and carry a gun was put into the battle. The Japanese officers told them it would be better to die in the attack rather than to be captured. At dawn over 3,000 troops charged forward in a final Banzai attack. They surged over the American lines causing 650 casualties; killed or wounded U.S. troops. Over 4,300 Japanese were killed, including many civilians. Saipan was declared officially secured on July 9. Admiral Namumo (the Japanese naval officer who led the carriers at Pearl Harbor and Midway) along with other Japanese officers committed suicide in a cave.

The Battle of Saipan resulted in a lot of bloodshed and loss of life. The record says that 3,400 American soldiers were killed and over 10,000 were wounded. Over 24,000 Japanese were killed in the three-week campaign for control of Saipan. Over 5,000 Japanese committed suicide by shooting themselves or jumping off a cliff into the sea rather than be captured. They considered it an honor to die for the Emperor of Japan. They were also brainwashed to believe they would be tortured if taken prisoner by the Americans. However, an unusual number of Japanese soldiers, 920 in all, did surrender and were taken prisoner. Those prisoners were being held in a high security compound on the southwest end of the island. Many civilians took their own lives, because of the warning by the Japanese about being tortured by the Americans. The death toll of civilians rose to 22,000.

The B-29 *Super Bombers* had been bombing Japan from China. The Army Air Corps needed Saipan to reduce the range for the bombers to only 1,200 miles. By the time my ship arrived, the United States had a fleet of several hundred bombers on Saipan.

Although Weithorn and I had been sent to different tent cities, somehow we were able to locate each other. In the evenings, after training exercises or after additional training, we could get permission to leave camp. When possible, we would go for some excursions around the island. We could catch a ride in military vehicles to explore the island, which was 10 to 12 miles long. It was 72 square miles altogether. On one of our trips we hitchhiked to the northern tip of the island where we saw some very nice homes that had escaped destruction during the battle. Those had been owned by the more affluent natives of the island. One of the drivers, who picked us up, told us those homes were now used to house U.S. military officers.

Being a Forestry Major, I found the many kinds of unusual vegetation and tropical trees fascinating. We passed an enormous building that had been destroyed, leaving twisted scorched steel behind. The jeep driver told us it had been a large sugar cane refinery; the main industry of the people before the Japanese took control of the island. The whole place was in total ruin from non-use and/or from hits during the bombing and shelling of the island.

Destruction from the bombing could be seen everywhere. We passed an abandoned tank still in the water on the beach where it stalled or was hit by some weapon. There was a machinery graveyard of discarded trucks, jeeps, and a variety of junk. The air force had a large airplane graveyard containing disabled planes. We saw several airplanes that had been scrapped. If an airplane failed to perform properly it was ditched rather than take time to repair it. They chose to use one that was operating successfully and safely. They did not want to chance a defective plane that might go down in enemy waters or over Japan, jeopardizing a mission. We really saw and learned a lot on that trip.

On a separate excursion, we traveled down to the beach and took a swim in the ocean. After our swim, we caught a ride over to the large U.S. Air Force base to watch the planes coming and going. There were several big B-17's at the base, which were used in making regular night raids on Japan. Those bombing runs met little resistance. The Japanese had lost about all their defensive capabilities by that time and were clearly losing the war. The planes were being loaded with fuel and bombs for that night's bombing mission over Japan. Herbert and I got the idea of seeing if one of the pilots would let us ride along on the mission. We should have known that was a foolish thing to do and even more ridiculous to ask. The answer to our inquiry was a flat "**NO!**" Actually, after we thought more about the danger involved, we felt rather relieved.

Trucks and Snails and Duck Landing Tales

After a few days of living in the tent city, one evening at mail call, an officer came into the area and asked if one of us would volunteer to ride on a water truck to help haul water for four days of the week. Again, I was the first one to yell, "Here!"

Naturally, I got the usual "boos" and taunts from those who thought it ridiculous to volunteer for any work. I laughed to myself about it. The next morning, I reported to the officer's tent to begin my new volunteer position. I thought riding around in the water truck was a fun job. It was much better than going out on the hillside for additional training or sitting around in the tents watching guys play cards, smoke cigarettes and tell dirty jokes. The driver was a sergeant who had been in the service for a while. He was an interesting guy to talk with. I listened avidly as he told of his many excursions in the army and of his life.

Our work entailed going to a large water tower to fill up the tank on the truck. Then we would deliver the water to the various tent cities. We supplied the kitchens and filled the canvas drinking bags that were hanging in convenient places for men to fill their canteens. That job lasted for most of the remaining time I was on Saipan, but it was not the only duty I had during that time.

In the army every soldier had to take his turn at KP or guard duty. In addition to my water delivery job, I was assigned to guard duty at the water tower for a 24-hour period. For two hours I stood guard at the tower. Another guard then relieved me, so I could rest or sleep for four hours. Once again, we rotated. In that way I stood watch four times during the 24-hour period. A large hill, that was just above the water tower, contained a thick jungle. It was known that some Japanese soldiers were hiding out there. They were the remnant, remaining after the U.S. Army took control of the island. They were very slick and could somehow sneak past the guards to get into the kitchen to steal food. That happened quite frequently and it seemed impossible to catch them.

The water tower was lit up with bright lights during the night. It was the guard's job to walk around the tower to guard it. It seemed to me that I would be a prime target for anyone who might come out of the jungle with a gun, or try to tackle me and take my gun. During my tour of guard duty, I would stay in the shadow of the water tower on the side away from the jungle so I could be concealed. From there I could look around either side of the tower to watch for any activity. I stayed out of the spotlight! When it was about time for the sergeant to bring the relief guard I would begin walking.

During some of the training sessions, we went out on a hillside to learn about possible situations that might be encountered in battle. We were to sit in groups on the ground to listen to an officer's instructions. It was difficult to find a place to sit without sitting on large snails. They were as big as a half-dollar coin and were everywhere!

The ground and the hills were covered with these snails. Saipan was rainy and humid which provided an environment conducive to an abundant snail population on all the hills and throughout wooded areas. The island was so torn up from the devastation of the war that little or no other wildlife remained.

On those hills were numerous concrete *pillboxes*. The structures were ten feet square and four feet high, with an opening on one side large enough for a person to crawl through. The structures were defense-hiding places for the Japanese. Evidently, they lived in those pillboxes for a period of time, judging by the piles of snail shells just outside the opening. Evidently, after eating the snails, they just pitched the empty shells out the opening. We learned that the Japanese did not feed their soldiers well and that their soldiers were hungry most of the time. We never did learn if they ate the snails alive or if they had a way of cooking them.

The empty pillboxes were utilized to demonstrate the use of the flamethrower. A soldier was to approach the opening of a cave or similar hideout under the support of machine gun fire. When the person operating the flamethrower was close enough to the shelter, the machine gun would stop. The flame operator would then shoot a 15-to-20-foot flame into the opening. Although we were not asked to actually practice that exercise, the operation and use of the flamethrower was taught and demonstrated to all of the infantrymen. It was alarming to watch and imagine the impact. Unfortunately, I would witness it in action later on.

On Oahu, we had used live ammunition on the firing range and practiced adjusting our gun sights to *zero* on the M-1 for good accuracy. On Saipan though, no live ammunition was used in our training, except for hand grenades, and that was strictly limited. The training practice was of utmost importance, to make sure we learned to pull that pin *only* when we were ready to get rid of the grenade. Then we had to learn how to throw it properly and take immediate cover.

On several days, different small groups of us were taken to a beach area where an officer explained the use of army ducks for bringing supplies from ship to shore. At other times these were used as landing craft for men on the initial invasion. While on that exercise the duck would be loaded with guys, taken a distance out to sea, then back to shore, as would be the case in an invasion. The driver of the duck was able to lower the tire pressure to enable traveling on the sandy beach and then inflate the tires for driving on a hard surface.

Retaking of Guam and Tinian

Soon after defeating the Japanese on Saipan, the Americans had invaded Guam, which was the largest of the three in the island group. Three days after Pearl Harbor in 1941, Japan had invaded Guam and taken it from the

United States. The Japanese maintained a garrison there as a defense of the island and their homeland.

The United States came back to haunt them on July 21, 1944, with an invasion force of 36,000 soldiers. The Japanese had 18,500 defenders. The landing was rough and treacherous, because of the island being surrounded with coral reefs and high cliffs. It was even more difficult to get supplies and equipment onto the island. As was always the rule of the Japanese, they were to *fight to the last man*, rather than surrender. Retaking the island of Guam cost the Americans 3,000 killed and 7,125 wounded. The island was secured on August 10. The Japanese had 18,000 of their own killed and 485 taken as prisoners. Most of the prisoners did not really surrender, but were wounded and taken captive by the Americans. The defeat on Guam was another real setback for the Imperial Headquarters in Japan.

During the operation of Guam 30,000 more Americans invaded Tinian, the third island of the Marianas. The approach to it was not quite as difficult, since it had a suitable beach where the landing craft could bring troops close to the shore. From there men and equipment could make an uninhibited approach to land. Less resistance was met and the Japanese were defeated in nine days. The Japanese had a total of 8,800 to defend the island. Eight thousand of those were killed and 313 were taken prisoner. The Americans had 328 killed and 1,570 wounded.

Now the United States had regained control of most of the islands that had been taken by the Japanese back in 1941 and 1942. General MacArthur had returned to the Philippines because the war was still raging there.

There was one final step before invading the homeland of Japan. That would be Okinawa. The Americans realized that Okinawa would be heavily fortified and extremely difficult to take. But, there could be no turning back. To stop before total victory would only allow the Japanese to rebuild their military machinery and initiate counter attacks to regain their losses.

By that time it should have been evident to the Imperial Headquarters in Japan that they were losing the war they had started! Many of their cities had been destroyed by U.S. bombing raids and they were still getting hit every day and night by our planes now coming from Guam and Saipan. Their armies were being defeated in every island battle and becoming seriously reduced in number. They had lost most of their air power and their ships continued to be sunk by our submarines. The Philippines was the only place where they were still holding out. They were no longer able to inflict damage to the Allies on any of the islands and definitely had not come close to reaching the United States with their war machinery. They had repeatedly been given the opportunity to surrender and stop the killing. Regardless of suffering defeat after defeat, Japan's leaders had decided to let the war eventually be fought in their homeland where they thought they could make a decisive stand and be victorious. The loss of the Mariana Islands was a severe setback to the Japanese.

Headline News!

During our time on Saipan, we received important news of various kinds; both of the war and other national news. The good news to reach us was that the war in Germany had come to an end! The United States, Great Britain and Russia had at last defeated the Germans, with the final surrender being May 7, 1945.

Also, we heard the sad news of the death of President Roosevelt that occurred on April 12! On that same day, an emergency cabinet session was called and Vice President Harry Truman was sworn in as president. He was immediately thrust into making some of the most crucial decisions affecting our nation!

Of course that made international news. We were saddened to hear of his death. It was shocking, causing anxiety and grief across the United States; indeed, around the world! Roosevelt's death was from a massive cerebral hemorrhage (a stroke). His family and those around him had done much to comfort him during his illness. Those closest to him had anticipated his death, but his failing health had not been made known to the general public. However, we knew our country had provisions for the vice president to immediately assume the powers of the president, so the transition would be smooth and the war effort would continue as before.

Japan's chief operating officer for Okinawa reported that the Japanese troops took it as glorious news. Their spirits were lifted, and they were led to believe that the death of our president would weaken us such that they might regain territories they had lost. Imperial Headquarters was ecstatic, thinking that the American troops would discontinue their attack on Okinawa and would leave the island. Their staff officers seemed convinced that now the Japanese would surely win the war. They did not realize that America was going to take Okinawa, whether or not the Japanese fought to the last man. America had gained superior air and sea power by that time. From then on, Japan never had a chance of winning. It was a ridiculous supposition to think the Americans would withdraw from that operation.

President Roosevelt had been in office for more than 12 years, longer than any other president. He was the only person in the history of our country that was ever elected for a fourth term as president. He had led the country through the crises in Europe to the defeat of Nazi Germany and was within sight of defeating Japan. Unfortunately, he did not live to see the victory and the end of World War II.

After a White House funeral on April 14, President Roosevelt was transported back to Hyde Park by train. He was guarded by four servicemen, one each from the Army, Navy, Marines, and Coast Guard. He was buried in the Rose Garden on the estate of the Roosevelt family home in Hyde Park on April 15.

The New York Times declared, "Men will thank God on their knees a hundred years from now, that Franklin D. Roosevelt was in the White House."

Shortly after Roosevelt's death, we learned about the death of Ernie Pyle, a nationally known war correspondent. He had closely reported war news throughout the days of World War II, from the time of the invasion of Normandy until the day of his death on April 18, 1945. He had started his writings about the Nazi bombings of London in 1940. Prior to that, he had worked on the *Indiana Daily Student* newspaper at Indiana University.

In 1923, he quit college a few months before graduating and soon had a job with *The Washington* (D.C.) *News*. During the following years, Ernie continued in the news publishing business and did some traveling until becoming a war correspondent.

In the fall of 1940 he claimed, "A small voice came in the night that he must go (to the war front in Europe)." He lived with the Yanks in foxholes and won the hearts of people by writing his firsthand accounts. He joined the soldiers at the invasion of Normandy and again wrote columns from his personal experience on the front lines, relating his own feelings and emotions as he watched the carnage. He wrote from his heart about seeing men wounded and dying. By interpreting the scene of the soldiers, his columns brought home the hurt, the horror, the loneliness, and homesickness of the soldiers. He never attempted to make war look glamorous...as he hated and feared it.

People back home eagerly read his columns in newspapers all over the United States. Even the generals and officials in Washington took note and appreciated the manner in which Ernie Pyle was bringing the news of the war to those at home, who were praying and working towards victory.

There was a time he was nearly killed by one of our own planes and told of the death and agony of others all around him. Then he confided to his millions of readers that he was going home.

"I don't think I could go on and keep sane," he wrote. "I am leaving because I have got to stop. I have had all I can take for a while."

He went home to his small cottage in Albuquerque, New Mexico, to be with "That Girl," as he called his wife. While there, he became very distraught over the progress of the war and the continual thought of the war front haunted him. He felt he had to go back. This time to the Pacific Theater. In January of 1945, he left for San Francisco. He was dreading it, as he despised what he had already seen of war. He also had a feeling that he may have used up all his chances. Nevertheless, he felt compelled to go. He claimed there was a war on and he was part of it. He wrote, "I'm simply going because I've got to."

He first went to Iwo Jima and followed the "doughboys" (this term was used prior to the usage of G.I.) into their foxholes. He continued writing his columns about the tragedies, suffering and situations–in the same way as he had done in France.

He moved on to Okinawa soon after the invasion began. He had joined headquarters in the island's chief town of Tegusugu, where it was presumed that the Marines had eliminated all the opposition. Ernie accompanied a commanding general, Coolidge, to observe conditions near Le Selma, an area on an island near Okinawa. As the vehicle reached a road junction, Japanese troops began firing a machine gun located on a coral ridge about a third of a mile away. The men stopped their vehicle and jumped into a ditch. Pyle and Coolidge raised their heads to look around for the others.

When they spotted them, Pyle smiled and asked Coolidge, "Are you all right?"

Those were his last words. The machine gun began shooting again and Pyle was struck in the left temple. (The Ernie Pyle State Historic Site in Dana, Indiana, contains a telegram from the government to Pyle's father, stating Pyle was killed by a sniper.) The colonel called for a medic, but none was present. It made no difference, Pyle had been killed instantly.

The commanding general reported his death, "I regret to report that War Correspondent Ernie Pyle, who made such a great contribution to the morale of our foot soldiers, was killed in the battle of Ie Shima today."

He was killed while with the commanding officer of the 77th Division of the United States Army. This was the division to which I was assigned just a few weeks later.

His father in Dana, Indiana, was quite shaken to hear the news, as was President Truman, and his many readers everywhere. For three years his writings had entered some 14 million homes...almost as personal letters from the front. He was buried with his helmet on, in a long row of graves among soldiers, with an infantry private on one side and a combat engineer on the other. At the 10-minute service the Army, Navy, and Marine Corps were all represented. Americans erected a monument to him at the site. When Okinawa was returned to Japanese control after the war, the Ernie Pyle monument was one of three American memorials they allowed to remain in place. Pyle's remains were later reinterred at the Army cemetery on Okinawa. Lastly, they were reinterred at the National Memorial Cemetery of the Pacific located in Honolulu. Pyle was among the very few American civilians killed during the war to be awarded the Purple Heart. This is noted on his gravestone.

News of *Victory Day* (Germany's surrender) came to the United States approximately four weeks after the death of President Roosevelt. Victory was exciting news all over the country and it was especially good news to us! However, several forces which did not surrender on May 7, 1945, surrendered piecemeal in the following days. Many units fighting in Europe did not have the news of Germany's surrender and continued to offer resistance here and there for several days, some surrendering as late as a week later.

In mid-May, the Japanese commanders on Okinawa became aware of that news and they were very much discouraged. They knew that Japan was doomed. They had lost their only ally and Russia had just invaded one of their islands. Japan was gearing up for a final decisive battle on the homeland, while leaving Okinawa in a totally hopeless situation. Imperial headquarters sent a report to boost the morale of their remaining troops on Okinawa, but it was of little encouragement. After the war, Japanese Colonel Yahara Hiromichi, wrote that it had been nonsense to continue the fighting and letting soldiers die for the purpose of leaders who wanted to preserve their own power and pride.

Germany had been fighting a defensive battle on many fronts since the invasion of Normandy by British and American soldiers in June of 1944. The Germans were losing but, like Japan, refused to surrender. Of course that is another story in itself. Commanders of most German forces obeyed the order to surrender that was issued by the German High Command but not all did so. The last battle of World War II in Europe ended May 20.

The end of the war in Europe was exciting news everywhere and certainly was international news. However, it could not be celebrated as the end of the war for the United States, because the war in the Pacific continued to bring sad news to the American people.

During the last months of the war in Germany and immediately following, Allied soldiers discovered a number of concentration camps. Those camps had been used to imprison and exterminate an estimated 11 million people. The imprisoned people consisted of Jews, homosexuals, Roman Catholics, various minorities and disabled persons. Additional political enemies, particularly Communists, formed over five million. The cruelty there was similar to the cruelty meted out by the Japanese to their prisoners. The American soldiers found deplorable conditions in those death camps and liberated the thousands who still remained alive.

Several Nazi leaders were tried and executed for war crimes. All of these important news items were of concern to us on Saipan, but our main concern was our next destination. The news we had heard about the invasion of Okinawa spoke of the struggles of the infantrymen on that island. No one was in any hurry to get there. I laid awake at night, troubled with thoughts of the unknown experiences ahead and dreading what awaited us.

Okinawa Bound

After about three weeks of living in our tent city (our "motel" as some called it), we received orders one day to pack up and get ready to ship out. Again, there was no mention of where we were going. We were well aware there was heavy fighting at that time on Okinawa; a place that was very unknown to us. While on Saipan, the news we got was that the Army and the Marines on Okinawa were meeting heavy resistance, resulting in many casualties. That was worrisome news! With those developments on our minds, we were transported under the cover of darkness to the harbor where six transport ships waited for us to embark.

The officers knew where we would be going, but it was considered vital not to disclose destination information. Reflecting back to Camp Blanding, the officers probably knew before we left there that the new trainees would be going to either Iwo Jima or Okinawa. We were to enter the final battle of the Pacific.

The day after we boarded, Herbert Weithorn and I were elated to discover that we were on the same ship! We considered it Divine providence and a blessing to continue our Christian friendship. It also helped us to take our minds off the dreaded certainty of our destination. Every one of us was traveling with a full battle pack, gas mask, rifle, field rations, mess gear, a small shovel, and our own personal casket! Each person had a small mattress cover in his pack that served as a body bag if he were killed. Ammunition was to be distributed only after reaching our destination and we were ready for action.

The convoy of six ships sat in the harbor of Saipan for five days with all the soldiers on board. Each transport probably had a thousand troops on board. We were not disappointed in the delay and would have been willing to remain there indefinitely. The bond of friendship developed closer between Herb and me with the extra time to chat, watch the scenery, and take our meals together below deck. They must have had a ton of food down at the kitchen because they fed us three hearty meals each day. The ocean breeze made a comfortable atmosphere for the card players and for others who just wanted to watch other ships going and coming near the harbor. Planes frequently went to the island. We could hear big B-17 bombers taking off on their night missions of bombing Japanese cities.

Finally, on the sixth day, the ships pulled out of the harbor and the island of Saipan became smaller and smaller, until completely out of sight. Then all we could see was the wide open expanse of water. I hoped we would not encounter any lurking Japanese submarines that could send us to the bottom of the sea.

During the next four days the ships traveled in what, I expect, was a regular ship convoy. They were in two rows at least 100 yards apart. While all ships were easily in seeing distance of each other, the distance between them (front and back) was considerable. Besides being watchful and alert, I wondered if there was always an uneasiness with the ship captain and the crew when traveling in enemy waters.

Time passed, just the same as before, with the routine of loafing on deck, sleeping, reading old magazines, playing cards, eating our meals, and just watching the waves. The men were a little somber at times and not quite the happy-go-lucky guys that had been traveling before. I think all of us were very much concerned about what our next landing would be like!

We finally reached a place in the ocean, while it was yet daylight, where we saw hundreds of ships and the shoreline of Okinawa. I had never seen so many ships in my entire life! I did not know the United States even had that many ships! There were battleships, aircraft carriers, transport ships, and hundreds of somewhat smaller ships, but they all seemed huge.

We did not know at the time that Japanese kamikaze planes and submarines had sunk some of our ships. Those were suicide planes and boats loaded with explosives. I am glad they did not tell us that disturbing fact. It's a good thing that at times we were not fully informed. What a terrible disaster it would have been for us, if they had piloted just one of those planes into one of our six ships loaded with soldiers!

CHAPTER FIVE

OKINAWA

Prepared, but not Ready

After the fall of the Mariana Islands, Saipan, Guam, and Tinian, the big military question was, which would be next, Okinawa, Formosa, or Taiwan? Okinawa was chosen, even though it was the most heavily fortified, because it was closest to the Japanese homeland and for several other strategic reasons.

The civilian population of Okinawa was estimated to be 500,000 people. The Japanese had ruled it a long time without allowing much development. It seems that they had kept the people in a primitive state of living and under much suppression. Yet, we are told that the civilians were contented with their simple way of life until the Japanese military started moving in to build their defenses, anticipating the inevitable attack by the Americans. Okinawa was actually a prefecture of Japan; a territory under their jurisdiction. As such, Japan could just move the military in without informing the residents. They told the Okinawans that they had come to protect them from the terrible Americans.

Japanese propaganda warned the Okinawan people that American soldiers would be very cruel to any who were captured. Under control of the Japanese army, the civilians lived very harsh and difficult lives. Thousands of men were conscripted into their army. Many others were forced into slave labor, fortifying the island against the inevitable invasion by the United States.

At the start, the total contingency of Japanese soldiers was over 80,000 men. Over 20,000 more were not actually from Japan, but were Okinawan farmers pressed into service, thus were of dubious combat material. Around 1,700 were high school boys, some as young as 14 years old.

Three airplane runways were built and caves in the mountains were developed into everything imaginable. The Japanese army headquarters, hospital facilities, barracks, and supply dumps would be housed underground in the caves. There was plenty of space for an abundance of food and other supplies in the caves. The Imperial Army wanted the soldiers to be fully supplied with everything needed to gain victory in the expected battle.

Much of the island was very mountainous, which served as defensive areas for the Japanese during the war. Those strong defenses resulted in considerable loss of life for the Americans attempting to reach the enemy holed up in the network of caves in the mountains. Interestingly, the Okinawans used the caves as burial places where the remains or bones were placed in large ceramic pots. Some of the guys wanted to investigate those pots but were not allowed to bother them. The network of caves they expanded throughout the mountain could hold thousands of troops and even large pieces of military equipment. The Japanese were planning to fight a war of attrition (wearing down the enemy by reducing their energy and resources). They made no plans for attacking the invaders. They would be hidden away in the caves and bunkers–letting the Americans come after them. They were convinced and determined that the Americans would be defeated by those tactics on Okinawa.

The United States had been making elaborate preparations for taking Okinawa. They had surrounded the coasts of Okinawa with 1,300 ships of all sizes, comparable to that employed for the Normandy invasion the previous summer. Along with the battleships, aircraft carriers, and various other ships, there were over 300 transport ships carrying 180,000 troops prepared for the invasion. The U.S. Army and Navy had compiled and maintained a supply line of 750,000 tons of supplies needed for that conflict. It is hard to comprehend a feat of assembling such a vast line of supplies.

Some have wondered why the date designated for the beginning of the campaign for Okinawa, known as Landing Day or L-Day, was chosen to be April 1, 1945. The cynics did not miss the significance of that being April Fool's Day. It was called *Operation Iceburg*.

The invasion began in the early hours with the first wave of 16,000 troops of the 77th Infantry Division going ashore. By nightfall, some 60,000 troops were ashore with little or no resistance.

Colonel Hiromichi Yahara escaped at the end of the battle. He wrote an account of the battle from the Japanese point of view some 30 years afterwards. He told of some officers standing with him on top of Mt. Shuri with binoculars watching the American troops coming ashore, bringing tanks, trucks, and other equipment onto their island. They chuckled with delight among themselves about the Americans' unexpected ease, as they came in unopposed. They were also thinking of the surprise they had in store for when the Americans began approaching their fortifications. Yahara and the generals did not agree with the Imperial Headquarters. He stated that he knew there was no way the Japanese would win the battle, but they had three reasons for holding out as long as possible.

First and foremost, to them it was a dishonor to surrender. It was more honorable to die for the Emperor, rather than be taken as a prisoner. Second, they needed to stall the Americans as long as possible, giving Japan more time to prepare for the invasion of the homeland, which they knew would be next. Finally, they wanted to inflict as much damage to the invading troops as possible, making them pay a supreme price for the island.

There had been several bombing missions against Okinawa as early as the previous October. The capitol city was almost totally destroyed. Some have wondered why was it so important to bomb the cities, causing so much loss of civilian life. Presumably, that was to reduce support lines to Japanese troops holed up in the hills. In the end, over half of the civilians of Okinawa lost their lives. Reconnaissance flights in September, before the bombings, had revealed that the fortifications were in the mountains.

During the first 24 hours of the invasion, 10 battleships and over 100 other ships had fired several tons of shells onto the island. Airplanes from the carriers had dropped bombs and strafed the island. One would think that no living thing could be left on the island. It was reported that many remaining civilians also took refuge in the caves. Most of the shelling and bombing had little effect on the soldiers, who were already hiding in the caves and fortified bunkers.

It is difficult to imagine the vast amount of supplies needed to support an army of a several thousand men at war. The army ducks were constantly busy hauling in supplies from the supply ships, which had no place to dock for unloading. At the staging area, and maybe at other places, there were huge stacks of food, ammunition, fuel barrels, and other supplies, which all had to be constantly guarded.

A large hospital tent had to be erected and supplied with cots, beds, tables and all kinds of medical equipment. Large refrigeration units had to be brought onto the island for perishable foods and hospital needs.

Almost six times as many soldiers were needed for support personnel, as were needed in the actual battle. There were transportation people, cooks, engineers, medical people, burial crews, navy men, and many other jobs that had to be performed to support the actual fighting men. Which meant that only about one in seven of the Americans on the island were actually in battle. That was typical of any place where the Americans were at war during WWII. It was probably about the same in wars that followed.

By the time we reached Okinawa, the Marines and Infantry divisions of the U.S. Tenth Army had accomplished the initial invasion and had taken control of the northern part of the island. They had also taken several outlying islands, airfields, and landing beaches. The Japanese had given little sign of their presence initially. Unknown to us, it was their plan to save their resources while luring the Americans toward the mountains where they could inflict heavy losses.

The island was swarming with army vehicles, while hundreds of ships and boats of all kinds were out at sea. However, our fleet of sea vessels were diminished by the Japanese kamikaze planes and submarines as they sank several of our ships.

Japanese Suicide Attacks Continued

At the close of Easter week, the Japanese attempted a major sea and air attack on the American fleet off the coast of Okinawa. They launched a two-pronged attack: a wave of suicide planes dubbed *Floating Chrysanthemums* and a flotilla of warships led by the *Yamato* (the Japanese super battleship and the world's largest). Most of the 700 suicide planes were shot down, but enough made it through to do considerable damage by sinking eight destroyers and smaller ships as well as damaging 10 others. More kamikaze planes would follow in later attacks. The kamikazes were responsible for a high rate of our naval casualties in the Battle of Okinawa.

The *Yamato,* as part of the suicide mission to help destroy the U.S. fleet, was expected to wreak heavy damage with its 18-inch guns. It was reported that the *Yamato* had been given enough fuel for a one-way trip. The sleek graceful ship was supposed to be the fastest ship in the world and had the world's heaviest naval guns. It was soon spotted and attacked by swarms of American aircraft carrier planes. She was hit by several torpedoes and bombs, then sank on the second day without ever getting off one shot with her big guns. All of the eight accompanying destroyers were also sunk by torpedo and bombs with only a few survivors. The crew of 2,800 on the *Yamato* was lost, except for some 200 who managed to escape and were rescued by American ships. The U.S. suffered the loss of 10 planes and 12 men in the sea battle against the *Yamato* and their destroyers.

Long Road to the Castle

The Japanese chose to establish a major defense line about five miles north of the Shuri Castle. It was called the *Shuri Defense Line*. The Shuri Castle was a 15th century fort that had once housed Okinawa's feudal kings. It was there that the Japanese command was positioned. The area around it was made up primarily of mountains with deep ravines that were difficult to scale but easy to defend. From those ramparts, they could chew up the American forces piece by piece as they tried to advance.

In the first part of May 1945, the Army's 77th Division was given the task of taking the Shuri Castle. The 305th, 306th, and 307th Infantry of the 77th Division relieved the invasion forces of the Tenth Army and began pushing south, down the middle of the island along Route 5 (the main highway). They had reached this point when I joined the 77th Division as a replacement.

Our ship reached Okinawa at the beginning of May and dropped anchor in the harbor, off the western coast, late in the evening. There was still a little daylight, enabling us to see that the harbor was teeming with ships. There were even ships far out at sea. We learned later that over 1,600 ships had surrounded the island, 18 were battleships.

Two big battleships that were a short distance out at sea frequently fired their big 16-inch guns. We could see the flames shooting out the end of the long barrels of the guns with each volley, followed by three big sounds...BOOM, BOOM, BOOM! We could hear a zinging noise as the rounds flew through the air, then a few seconds later there were three loud explosions, which sounded like thunder. Those volleys of shots were repeated about every 20 or 30 minutes. At the same time other battleships were firing from different locations around the island.

That was my first impression of war—the image of the ships and the reverberating sound of their big guns. I could not help thinking that with each explosion some Japanese lives were taken…soldiers who had people back in Japan who loved them but would never see them again.

The realization of war hit me as I thought of people being killed with each of those firings. There was a feeling of regret that we had to kill people, yet I knew it was the only way to defeat the enemy. Japan had started the war. They refused surrender! The United States had no choice but to defeat them in order to avoid advances into free countries with their dictatorship and cruelty.

If Japan had surrendered at any time, the United States would have stopped the shooting, bombing and killing. Leaflets in their native language had been dropped, over and over again, offering an opportunity for leaders and individuals to surrender. Most people there desired an end to the killing, but surrender was not part of their culture.

The U.S. Army and Marines had already made the treacherous beach landings and had been on the island several weeks prior to my arrival. Along with hundreds of other soldiers I had arrived there to take part in whatever action was required of me. At some point that night we arrived, an announcement came for everyone to go over the ship's rail onto the rope ladders and climb down to landing boats below. We began climbing down the 30-foot rope ladders that hung over the side of the ship. Each man carried a full 50-pound pack on his back. The backpack contained half of a tent, ammunition, a gas mask, field rations, small shovel, poncho, blanket, a minimum of extra clothing, and a few other essentials. In addition, he had a 10-pound M-1 rifle slung on his shoulder. Most guys made it just fine, but one got about halfway down, lost his grip and fell. Fortunately, he landed on his back. The blanket in his pack, along with others in the boat trying to catch him, cushioned his fall. The reason for rope climbing practice in basic training was made abundantly clear. The landing boats then carried us to small temporary docks. I was glad it was there, instead of a place where we would have been forced to wade in the water to get ashore. Herbert and I lost each other in the throng of soldiers climbing off that ship and I wondered if he was there somewhere or if he had been sent to another area.

[A.E. Willis Illustration]

Once on the dock, officers started marching us in groups, up a road inland–to where we did not know. The island was approximately 130 miles long (from southwest to northeast) but of course we had no idea of our position or our final destination. We marched in silent apprehension for about three hours. Mile after mile, our weary feet carried us while the packs on our backs seemed to get heavier with each step. They halted us to rest only a couple of times. We were happy for those short rests. What a relief to unburden ourselves of the weight we were carrying. We were more relieved when we were ordered off the road at a staging area used for stockpiling supplies and assembling soldiers for battle.

Everyone was so weary, but we were not allowed to rest yet. We were told to pair up and pitch our pup tents. That did not merely mean assembling a tent. To do it correctly there was also digging to do. Calling upon our last reserves of energy, a friend (all soldiers were buddies) and I got out our half tents. Put together they made one full pup tent. We staked it down and went to our packs for shovels. As per previous instructions, we began digging a trench all the way around the tent. It was precautionary, in case of rain. If done properly it would carry away any water, keeping the inside of the tent dry, should it rain during the night. At long last we crawled thankfully inside. We arranged our blankets, used our packs as pillows, and fell into an exhausted sleep. Later in the night, the sound of heavy rain beating against our tent and drumming the ground outside awakened me.

Still snug and dry under my blanket, I prayed to remain so and that our trench would be sufficient! As we all were thoroughly spent from the lengthy march, most guys had not bothered to dig a trench. In the morning, those who had neglected to dig their trenches came dragging their sorry selves out of their tents. Everything was drenched! Clothes, backpacks and blankets–all were soggy! The trench had saved the night for my buddy and me. No water got in our tent and all our supplies were dry. How glad we were that we had forced ourselves, exhausted as we were, to go that *extra mile* and dig our trench before bedding down for the night.

Despite the continued chill drizzle of rain we were required to answer roll call and then take our mess gear to breakfast. It was served in the open field kitchen. I was not much of a coffee drinker but the wonderful aroma was so welcoming and tantalizing. That morning the hot coffee tasted really good! It was served in our big individual aluminum canteen cups. I must have developed a taste for it, as I consumed many more cups of it during the two days that we were in that staging area. It was somehow comforting and satisfying.

A chaplain that was there spoke with the group and had prayer with us each day. As infantrymen we well knew with certainty, that according to the heavy losses of men in the earlier battle, some of us would not return. At other sessions, we were briefed about the situation, informed of the rules and given instructions.

We were permitted to leave our area to explore some of the devastated areas nearby. Our excursions were permissible within limits and regulations set by the officers. We were told to carry our rifle at all times and to travel in groups of two or three for our safety. Three of us took advantage of that opportunity and went exploring. One of the guys was Bill Wheeler. We had been assigned together in the same hut during basic training at Camp Blanding, Florida. After that excursion I never saw him again.

That was the way it was with so many young men being thrown together and moved around. All were far from home, friends, and family, so new acquaintances quickly became friends. Then, there would be a move and you never knew if you would see that person again. It was always such a joy to meet up again with someone from a previous assignment. That was the case with my friend Herbert. I had neither seen him nor heard news of him, since we were sent different directions upon arriving at Okinawa, but I always knew there could be the chance of finding him again. I hoped it would be the case.

There had been many rice paddies and sugar cane fields. On that excursion, we saw torn up fields ravaged with bomb craters and destroyed buildings. Native Okinawans were wandering along traveled paths begging for food or tending rice paddies. Others seemed to just be going across small fields. We came upon some elderly women carrying heavy baskets on their heads. One woman was having a difficult time getting low enough for her basket to pass under a telephone wire that was strung across the field. I used the end of my rifle to raise the wire, so she could pass under it. She tried to bow and express her thanks to me as best she could with the load on her head.

Initially, the Okinawan people feared the American soldiers because of Japanese propaganda that called Americans "barbarians and devils". The Japanese further spread fear among the Okinawan people by telling them that the Americans would commit wholesale slaughter and grind up their remains for dog food. Although our army provided protected compounds for displaced residents, some preferred to live in their own improvised shelters.

In the camps and processing centers the Okinawans soon learned the truth about the Americans. They benefited from getting medical attention. Food was also being distributed to this population that had suffered deprivation from the Japanese in order to support the Japan war machine. They had long been treated as inferiors by the Japanese. Therefore, what they felt toward their former rulers was much fear and very little loyalty. After receiving considerate treatment they came to respect Americans.

The ravages of war could be seen everywhere! I never saw anything that looked like an actual road in the areas where we were. In a few places, what passed for roads were only small cart trails. Most of what remained on the island has been devastated. There were hills with craters and caves, devastated rice paddies and rutted narrow dirt roads. Everywhere were ruined huts of shattered settlements. Many islanders were killed, others were displaced. I had never before seen such devastation as I did during that excursion. By the looks of the remains, it appeared that there had once been beautiful areas with trees, as well as fields with cane and other vegetation. The ravages of war had damaged many trees and left things in a terrible condition. It was sad seeing the simple homes and villages destroyed.

We passed through a small bombed out village of six or seven buildings, a couple of which appeared to have been businesses. Much debris was scattered about and some papers had Japanese writing on them. I picked up an envelope and some paper with a Japanese letterhead on it, thinking it would be interesting to the folks back home. When I put it in with my next letter, the *oriental* stationery did not pass the censors and was sent back to me!

Walking back to camp along an old cart trail, we met three elderly men. They quickly hunkered down low in an offset place in the trail, as if they were afraid of us. I was whittling on a piece of wood with my scout knife. Suddenly it occurred to me that they were afraid of me with my knife out like that. I stopped in front of them, folded the knife and shook my head *no* while making other motions indicating that we did not mean any harm. We even gave them one of our field ration bars. We were rewarded with big smiles, and the men bowed to us several times as we went on our way. In that way we let them know we wanted to be friends, not enemies. We were glad to make it back to the *normality* of camp in time for supper.

Upon arrival at our staging area, we saw the Army engineers at work on Route 5 that went through the middle of Okinawa. As we progressed toward the front, we saw that the engineers were working close behind the infantrymen, as they pushed forward against the Japanese. The Army engineers were busily building a good road on the heels of our advancing army.

Battlefields consumed the land while the whole island was being taken over by the U.S. Army and Marines. As had been the case on all the other islands that were taken in the war, the land was used for building the much-needed roads, hospitals, cemeteries, tent cities, airfields, motor pools, and stockpiles of supplies. We were told that the capitol city was practically all destroyed, but I was not in that area any time to see it. In time of war there was no recognition of personal ownership of any of the lands. Sadly, the Okinawan civilians were caught in the crossfire of war. They suffered at the hands of both armies. The Japanese had deprived and enslaved the people, as the Americans rolled across their land.

Changing Out and Paring Down

On May 8, the third morning in that encampment, we assembled for marching orders. A couple of days had been spent there preparing to go to the battlefront. The cooks had served up some especially good meals during that time. The day before we were to move out we were given a supply of extra field rations to carry with us. We loaded up with water, field rations, hand grenades and ammunition. We were informed that we were getting new rifles and we were not going to need our gas masks. We had carried the gas masks the entire distance from Saipan for nothing, it seemed. Still, it was a relief to give them up, both for not having to use them and it lightened our load somewhat.

Trading out the rifles brought mixed emotions. Many did not like the new rifles, because we were accustomed to the M-1 and knew all about it from basic training. It could be somewhat unsettling to exchange the familiar for the unfamiliar. Into a truck we chucked our gas masks and exchanged our M-1 rifles for carbines. Admittedly, they were smaller and easier to carry. Before we moved out the chaplain read a few verses of scripture and had a few words of encouragement for our group. He prayed to God for our courage and success as we went forward into battle.

None of us were yet assigned to a company; all were lined up and joined with other groups marching in columns of two that must have stretched to a half mile long. Because of the rain, our road was a trail of mud that came high up on our combat boots. The extra weight of the mud made for an exhausting march. It clung to our boots so with each step we collected a little more and a little more of that trail, until it felt as though we were walking in buckets of lead. Nothing moved easily in that muck. Several army vehicles were stuck in the mud and were being pulled through with tanks and caterpillar tractors. It reminded me of the Beckville Hill Road, back home, when it was muddy. That trail may have been a section of Route 5, the island's main north-south highway. On the straight stretches of road, I attempted to see the end of that long line of men, but it stretched as far as the eye could see in both directions. I was never able to see the end, either in front or in back.

We went through a wooded area and passed by several dead Japanese soldiers lying scattered around among the trees. They were repulsive, swollen up like dead animals and still in full uniform. It was a hideous sight! The American burial crews had not yet reached the area to pick them up. As I looked at all those dead bodies, I could not help thinking how their loved ones back in Japan would never see them again, as would be the case for those Americans whom they had killed.

That was my first sight of the finality and horror of death in war. It was a shocking awakening that this was no longer training. It was real, and it was here. Our battle was not far ahead.

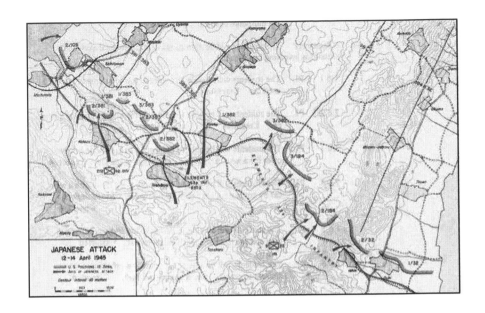

Assignment and Surprise

At long last, our mud weary march ended at the foot of a high hill not far from the front lines. The 77th Division had set up a command post there, in the area near Urasoe-Mura, where Route 5 bulges around a very steep slope. At that time, the Tenth Army was in a position less than 10 miles from the Shuri Defense Line. The Tenth Army stretched across the island west to east as follows: the Sixth Marines on the west coast, the First Marines inland, the 77th Division down the spine and the 96th Division on the eastern coast. The 305th Infantry of the 77th Division was positioned west of Route 5, next to the First Marine Division. The 307th Infantry of the 77th Division straddled Route 5 and the 306th Infantry of the 77th Division was to the east alongside the 96th Division.

The officers began sending us in different directions to be assigned to a company. We were then divided up into small groups with a sergeant in charge of each group. As I looked around those assigned to my group, there to my great delight and surprise was Herbert Weithorn! It had only been three days since we had been separated, but under these circumstances one never knew when the last time a friend's face would be seen. We were so happy to be in the same squad of Company C of the 77th Infantry Division. Those of us arriving were then mixed in, as replacements, with the soldiers who were already there.

As we were resting, a lieutenant came over to our group to tell us what to expect and what the battle situation was. He told us to pay special attention to those few soldiers who had combat experience. Those who had been in battles were spread throughout the companies to help the rookies learn how to keep their heads in battle. Figuratively and literally! The comment from the lieutenant, which stands out the most in my memory, was what he said about himself. He told us that he was one of us and was risking his life in this cruel war–just like us! "You do not salute me here," he said. "Do not address me as *Sir*. You only call me Joe and I don't wear my official bars or other insignia to identify me as an officer. That would make me a prime target for the enemy." He also advised, "Go sparingly with your field rations, because we never know how soon to expect a new supply. Sometimes, an army truck with the kitchen staff will bring a hot meal as close to the front as possible, but we can't depend on it."

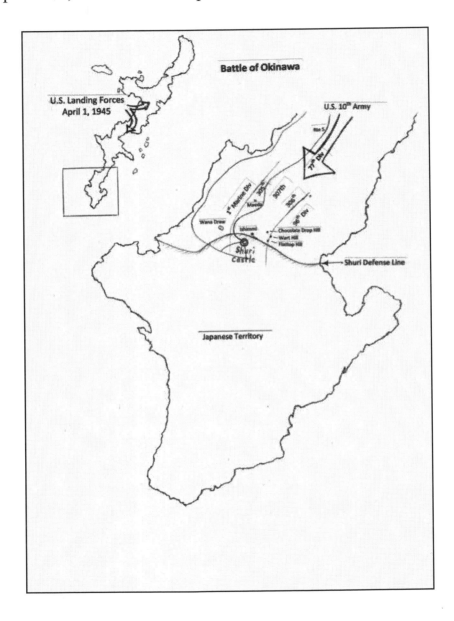

In the Trenches

After our briefing the lieutenant informed us, "Sergeant Tate will take you to the top of this large hill, which is actually the front line of our advance at this time. There you must dig your foxholes and follow his instructions about taking turns at guard duty throughout the night. Be ready to move out of those foxholes any time upon the sergeant's command."

Along the way up that hill we saw more dead Japanese. The hill had been taken in a previous battle. When we reached the top we were to hold the position. We were to defend it against any Japanese counterattacks, which they had done in other locations.

Once there, two other soldiers and I dug our first foxhole with a real purpose, in preparation for any possible advance of the Japanese. Here again, basic training had readied us for that moment. Every soldier carried a small shovel on his backpack for that very purpose. A foxhole consisted of two pits dug in a V-shape connected together, each one long enough for a man to lie down in. The front of the sleeping trenches met a deeper hole, which was dug so one soldier could sit while on watch. It provided for two guys to sleep in the long trench. There would be two-hour watches, then one of the other guys would be awakened to take a turn at the watch. In that way, one-third of the company was awake and on guard at all times during the night. The exchange of guard duty would extend throughout the day if necessary.

During that night, there was a continuous barrage of artillery firing overhead from our big guns in the rear. Mortar crews kept firing short-range rocket explosives at enemy positions. In addition, flares were fired to keep the area lit up so we could see any approaching enemy.

On that first night in the foxhole, I never slept a wink because of the noise, the lights, and the anxiety of the situation. However, on the following night and thereafter, I could lie there on that hard ground in the foxhole and sleep like a log during my four hours. I carried my little New Testament to read when possible and I prayed much while in those foxholes. I kept hoping the Japs were not making any offensive moves. There was no attack on our position. Maybe they were preoccupied with hiding in the caves to protect themselves and waiting for us to come after them. Perhaps the continuous bombardment with flares keeping the area lit up proved to be a deterrent from any night attack.

We learned that on a hill in another location, the Japanese did make a desperate mass counter attack, which was called a *banzai* attack. Over 1,000 Japanese barged down the hill screaming and waving assorted weapons. When that happened considerable loss of life among our soldiers was inevitable. The Japanese losses were higher as they expected to lose every one of their soldiers in the attack. It was a desperate move of sacrificing more of their soldiers in order to do as much damage as possible. The Japanese officers had little regard for the loss of life, even in their own ranks. All of the Japs were slaughtered in that attack, and several Americans were killed. Fortunately, my company was never involved in one of those attacks during the time I was with them.

The Japanese were, for the most part, making us come after them, but several times throughout the battle one of their officers would decide to make a counter charge with a mass of soldiers just to see how much damage he could do to the Americans. The Japanese soldiers were especially skilled at hand-to-hand bayonet combat. They were well trained for that, and those kinds of attacks were successful in driving our troops back. Their charge usually killed many of our soldiers, as the masses swarmed out overwhelming them. But in the end our machine guns and tanks would destroy the Japanese attackers.

Caissons Keep Rolling Along

Evidently the Japanese were not interested in retaking the hill our company was on, so we moved toward the next hill with practically no resistance. There we again dug foxholes. From that point we could see soldiers on a distant hill, which we assumed to be Japanese. Our tanks were firing point blank into the hillside, where they could be seen in a cave opening. We were allowed to fire our guns at the hill if we chose to do so. I think we were out of range for them to fire at us but we remained in the foxholes for safety. We walked around and over several enemy bodies that lay in a ditch just below the small hill on which we were situated. The stench was so bad that some guys shoveled dirt down the hill just to cover them up. From there we moved up to the next hill. In that move we came under some sniper fire. By crouching low and hitting the ground occasionally, we finally reached a position to where we could dig in. Our artillery and machine gun fire had eliminated most resistance on that hill. As a result, there were piles of dead Japanese soldiers to be seen.

After a few more days the officer took our company back to a rest area where we could sleep in an "outdoor hotel" (our pup tents) for one night and enjoy a hot meal. That was timely, because we were about to run out of field rations.

At one point, on our return back to the front, we stopped and the officer in charge explained to us how an artillery attack might actually be ineffective on the caves inside which the Japs were hiding. In order to do any real damage the artillery or machine guns would need to fire directly into the cave. Without a direct hit, they could retreat deep into the cave and be safe. The only solution was to use a flamethrower. The flamethrower consisted of a tank of fuel with a hose connected to the bottom. The operator strapped the tank onto his back and would ignite the fuel coming out of the hose while using it. When the operator squeezed a lever on the hose, a flame would shoot out 15 to 20 feet. The operator would have to sneak up close to the cave opening, while a machine gun team covered him by firing into the opening. That forced them to retreat to the interior. Then the flamethrower could advance close enough to the cave to shoot flames into the cave. What a horrible thought! But under the circumstances, our army could not advance in the face of continual Japanese fire from the cave. Although the flame might not reach some of those further back in the cave, many would suffocate from the smoke and fumes.

The captain asked for a volunteer to carry the flamethrower. That was one time that I did NOT volunteer!! Since he could not get a volunteer, he began looking around for someone to draft. I stared down toward the ground to keep from looking at him. I did not want that hideous job! I looked to see who the captain had picked. The young fellow that was selected had tears welling up in his eyes. He knew, as well as we did, that it was almost like a death sentence to get up close enough to a cave opening to do any good.

We were transferred to a few different holding positions within a couple of days, which were merely guarding positions. Even so, we understood that we were actually on the front lines. At each location we quickly dug our foxholes and experienced the same overhead artillery and flares at night. At times one of our tanks would lumber up close to us and fire several shots into the hills, directly in front of us, which were still occupied by the Japanese. We had not seen enemy soldiers except the dozens of dead ones which lay along our route–in shell craters and at the foot of our hill positions. Of course, there were those at distant cave openings that were no threat to us. Seeing those dead soldiers was a disturbing sight, even though they were our enemy and out there to kill us. There simply was no time for the American army to bury their dead properly, much less the enemy's dead. Our men had to be identified in order to notify their next of kin. A burial place was prepared for our soldiers on the island. That cemetery exists, yet today, on Okinawa. The question that hung ever present in our minds was always if or when a bullet would have our name on it.

The slowness of our advance south from hilltop to hilltop was due to the defensive positions the caves provided for the Japanese army. They were extremely hard to spot until you were almost upon them, and their snipers made very effective use of that concealment. Each of the hills was given an official designation, which the commanders used to direct our movements and monitor the battle.

One was *Chocolate Drop Hill*, which was taken in the face of heavy resistance, by the 306th Infantry of the 77th Div. That took place from May 11 through May 14, according to Army records of the Battle of Okinawa.

As was their tactic, the Japanese remained holed up in caves on the side or the foot of the mountains. Our tanks and machine guns would fire heavily into one of the caves at the side of the mountain. The soldier with the flamethrower was ordered to approach the cave from one side as instructed. When the soldier was within the proper distance, the volley of firing stopped, so that he could shoot flames into the cave. That eliminated enemy resistance from the cave making it possible for us to advance to the top of the hill.

My outfit was somewhere in the vicinity of Chocolate Drop Hill during that time. In the fighting, the 306th would advance, often as far as reaching the peak of a hill during the day. But during the night the Japs launched counterattacks with artillery, mortars, and buzz bombs, forcing the 306th back to safer lines. This "seesaw" continued for days.

On one of the days that we were dug into a hillside, we saw one of our fighter planes explode and burst into flames in the sky near us. Helplessly, we watched as the remains of the plane and the pilot tumbled to the ground. We were prevented from investigating, although the command post did send a detail to check the wreckage when it could be safely done.

On May 14, the 306th Infantry, led by five tanks, attempted to move in a southerly direction away from Wart Hill in a flanking movement around Chocolate Drop. Our company was running seriously low on field rations, so instead of moving up, we were taken back to a rest area. For one welcome night we could sleep in our pup tents and get a couple of hot meals. Everyone was looking forward to it...our morale was greatly lifted. The rest area was located approximately a mile behind the front lines. For the first time in days, we didn't have to dig a foxhole or sleep in a trench. The rest area was a field littered with hundreds of pup tents. The amenities included a good hot meal and nobody shooting at you.

We thoroughly enjoyed a big supper served up by the field kitchen. It provided a pleasant respite from the constant nerve shattering gunshots of the front lines. Then before our meal was finished two extremely jarring things happened. A single gunshot sounded very close by. It was so unexpected that we all jumped when we heard it. What enemy had approached that "safe" rest area? Soon we learned that a soldier had shot himself in the foot. He claimed it was an accident, but many suspected he did it to keep from going back to the front. If so, it was a cowardly act, but possibly it was his clever way of staying alive.

No sooner had we relaxed from that alarm, when another shot was heard! Now what? A Jap had come running into our camp! It is possible that he may have intended to surrender. It is also possible he was another one of those kamikazes with an explosive strapped to his body. If he had wanted to stay alive, running into the camp like that was not a smart way to do it. The men in the camp were more than a little edgy from being repeatedly shot at and targeted by Japanese artillery for days on end. Taking no chances, an officer immediately shot him.

After breakfast at the field kitchen on May 15, our company commander led us back south, toward the front lines near Ishimmi. On our way we met extremely exhausted and distraught returning companies. Their descriptions of the terrible situation ahead created considerable anxiety among our company. We were not left in doubt as to what lay ahead for us. The sight of the several burned out caves that we passed only served to add to the apprehension. The hills along Route 5 were riddled with those interconnected caves, where the Japanese army could be hiding. Many of the caves were originally Okinawan burial chambers. It was an Okinawan custom to dig burial vaults in the hillsides for interning their family members. Before the war, those burial sites were meticulously cared for and beautifully decorated. The Japanese army used those vaults for hiding places, storage for weapons and ammunition, and to be used as escape routes. Sometimes, the human remains inside the vaults had been scattered or removed so the chambers could be enlarged or connected to a network of other caves and burial chambers.

To give an idea of the scope of those tunnels, there was an instance where a tank fired six rounds of phosphorus shells into a cave to flush out the Japs hiding inside. Fifteen minutes later, observers reported seeing smoke coming from over 30 hidden openings on the slope. To say the caves were a perilous problem for the American soldiers would be an understatement!

Dread and Deliverance

Late the next afternoon we reached our position on the front lines again, a little to the east of Ishimmi. We advanced to an open area slightly behind a knoll and some trees. From there, the captain sent our squad of 12 men to scout ahead over the knoll to find where the Japs were hiding. I dreaded that because of the danger, but I went. No one ever disobeyed orders! We had moved out some distance from the company, when we were suddenly pinned down by heavy fire. Fortunately, there was a partial enclosure close to us, which was the remains of a former hut. A pile of timber and stones lay inside, which we used for cover. The rubble looked like it had been somebody's home before artillery reduced it to rubble. All that was left was the outline of a stone foundation, the broken stubs of walls, and mounds of rock and stone. We scrambled to find protection in the ruins, as bullets went flying around us. We had been blessed that nobody got hit. I crouched behind a big stone slab that looked fairly safe. The sergeant started yelling at me with some choice foul words, ordering me to get away from that cussed stone!

Quickly I dove behind another pile of debris. Only seconds later that slab was splattered with a hail of bullets. The sergeant saw the danger that I had not! He saved my life! In the bitter irony of war, he was shot through the forehead a few days later.

We were still pinned down when darkness began closing in. To stay there through the night would be a death sentence for all of us. The sergeant laid out a plan for us to fall back. One at a time, we darted into a nearby ditch where we could scoot on our belly for a distance and then crawl around a knoll toward our company. Every one of us reached a safe area and met up with the others of Company C without any casualties. During that action, I was sorry to find I had lost the scout knife that Dewey Hawes had given me back in Petersburg. But it was far better to lose the knife than to lose my life.

The rest of the company was already in their foxholes, so my squad got busy. We still had to dig our holes for the night. The captain had decided we were close enough to the enemy for the time being. During that night, and at other times when lying in the foxhole, a feeling of dread would come over me. It was the thought of emerging from that "comfortable bed" and facing the gunfire on the next hill. Like other soldiers, I did not want to die there on Okinawa. Yet we very well knew there was a real possibility of that, simply because the Japs were out there and they were determined to get as many of us as possible.

The next morning, on May 16, the captain sent a smaller group to scout out the enemy positions again. This time he chose six of us. Everyone knew the Japanese were up on the next hill. It seemed like an unnecessary risk, but we did as we were told. That time a tank led the way to protect us. Again, we came under fire at about 100 yards and our squad leader got shot through the abdomen from side to side. He was in terrible pain! The tanker called for a medic with a stretcher to carry him back. Two medics ran forward with a stretcher, gave the wounded man a shot of morphine and carried him back.

The tank driver asked where we were to go but without our squad leader, none of us knew. Venturing out in the face of open fire seemed too dangerous, without knowing where to go or what to do. I told the tank driver we ought to turn back before more of us got hit. He took my suggestion and we pulled back, crouching beside the tank keeping it between the Jap's guns and us. We made it back to the company without anyone else being shot.

While we were waiting for our next orders, we got word that a hot meal might make it up to us later in the day. That was a boost to everybody's mood. We were almost out of water as well, and with the news of replenishment, most of the men unwisely used what little water they had left. The hot meal and the water never did get there! The fruitless waiting for the food and water was the highlight of the day.

Gunfire and explosions could be heard in the distance. Occasional tanks would appear within our sight and would fire point blank into the hills ahead, which were still held by the enemy.

To the east of us was a hill called *Flattop Hill,* which the 307th Infantry was preparing to assault. Slightly to the south of Flattop was *Dick-Able Hill,* which had been in a bitter struggle for several days. We could hear constant gunfire and explosions coming from those areas.

The Bullet with My Name on It

The evening of the 16th was planned for a rifle platoon from Company D to join up with Company E of the 307th Infantry Division, for an attack on Ishimmi Ridge. This was located just east of the village of Ishimmi. The maneuver was scheduled to take place the next morning. By the end of the day it became clear that our hot meals were not coming. Perhaps worse, neither was our supply of water. That caused some grumbling, yet it was a minor annoyance compared to what was in store. At four o'clock the following morning, B Company came through our lines (Company C) on their way to make an attack on the next hill. On that same morning, the combined group of platoons from Companies E and D launched their ill-fated attack on Ishimmi Ridge, adjoining Shuri Ridge. That was getting close to Shuri Castle.

We felt really bad for those guys going out there, because it was inevitable some of them were going to lose their lives. I was glad that it was not Company C. But at the same time, I realized that we would probably be in the next wave. I prayed for those guys making that attack! I could not understand why so many of the guys would curse and use the Lord's name in vain, when at any moment, they might be seeing Him face to face. Our lives were at stake most of time. In those battle areas we would often see helmets with bullet holes through them. What they represented and the finality of it was a very disturbing sight.

The captain gave me his radio receiver to listen for messages coming through for him. I was to keep him posted on the events as I heard them. From the moment I got on the radio I heard nothing but bad news. Things were not going well for the soldiers who led the attacks that morning. I could hear that there was considerable resistance from the Japs. All morning and afternoon I heard pleas for help! There were cries for needed supplies, medics, and reinforcements. They were running low on ammunition and having a very hard time. Rather than continually relaying information to the captain, I finally just handed him the radio receiver.

An account, written after the war, reveals the terrible outcome of the assault on Ishimmi Ridge by the combined troops of Companies E and D. By 10 am almost all members of their machine gun crews had been killed. Of all the mortars, only one light mortar remained, and out of the five radios they started with, only one remained operable. As the morning wore on, the Japanese closed in on them. At least three bayonet charges were repulsed by grenades and many casualties were taken. The medic, although he was wounded, continued giving aid until his supplies ran out. [*77th Division History*, by Paul Leach]

Around noon a soldier came running into our area, exhausted from a long run, with terrible news. He sat down and cried aloud like a child about the loss of almost all his crew. He could hardly tell us what happened between sobs. I had never seen a grown man cry so hard. When he finally got his composure, he asked for water but none of us had any left. There was an old open well or waterhole nearby that had some murky water in the bottom along with dead twigs, leaves and other trash. He was so desperate for water that he dipped his canteen down into the hole trying to get at the water. Some guys tried to get him to wait a while, since water was expected to arrive at any time. He said, "I can't wait! I have to have some water!" All of us wanted water, but we were not as desperate as he was.

In the afternoon of May 17, 1945, the captain asked for volunteers to accompany a tank in an effort to rescue as many of the wounded men as possible. As usual I was ready, but not eager, to volunteer if I could help in anyway. While standing there by the tank, waiting for volunteers and draftees, I felt something slam into my left shoulder! The force of the thud knocked me to the ground. I realized that I had been hit!

[A.E. Willis Illustration]

It stunned me, but I remember my first thought was, "Now I get to go home and get out of this situation." Pain had not set in, so I didn't know whether my wound was serious. When I felt blood running down my arm, I realized that I ought to summon the medic sitting about 20 feet from me. I motioned for him to come to me. He said, "No, you come here." He did not want to get in the line of fire. All who could, were quickly in their foxholes by now! The captain and the other guys took cover behind the tank.

When I tried to crawl to the medic it caused too much pain in my shoulder, so I jumped up and ran to him. I thought surely I had a fracture of some kind. After my jacket and shirt were removed, I could see blood spurting out with each beat of my heart, from the bullet hole in the front of my shoulder.

Knowing the danger of losing a lot of blood, I put my finger on the hole to stop the flow. I told the medic to patch the hole in my back, while I held my finger on the front one.

The medic had some kind of powder that he put on my wound to stop the bleeding. After he finished on the backside of my shoulder, he stopped the bleeding of the wound in front and gave me a shot of morphine. Then he helped me put my shirt back on and draped the shirt over my left shoulder. By fastening the lower button on my shirt, it became a makeshift sling. He helped me with my jacket, then showed me a trail and said, "Just keep going, there will be plenty of guys back that way to direct you to a first aid station."

I left my rifle and backpack with all my belongings and started walking down the narrow trail, shaken but alive. Maybe it was the morphine, or the shock, but I was so relieved at leaving the front lines that I hardly felt any pain in my shoulder. The thought of getting to leave that place overshadowed everything in that moment. I felt God had spared my life for some reason. I had often prayed that God would spare me from having to pointblank shoot at another person, which He did. I was wounded…but I was *walking*.

About 100 yards down the trail, I came upon another soldier from a different platoon in our same company. He had been shot in the left leg and was struggling along, making very slow progress. I let him hold onto my right shoulder so he could hop on his good leg. I never even thought to ask his name or how he got hit. Helping him was the need of that moment! We came upon a four-man mortar station and decided to stop there for a rest. We were both very thirsty and asked if they had any water. They let us have all the water in their canteens, because they knew that we had lost blood and needed water. We gladly drank from their canteens. They would be able to get more. My companion and I had run out of water long before. The two days we had been at the front had depleted our canteens. The mortar team even emptied their canteens into ours so we would have water to continue our walk.

They told us which way to go and how to find the road to the field aid station. We resumed our slow hobble down the trail. We found the road, more like a dirt path, cut into the side of a big hill. We turned north and had gone only a few yards when suddenly an explosion went off only a few yards downslope from us. We were knocked to the ground. I tried to recall if I had heard the telltale thrumming of an incoming artillery shell. It seemed that we had heard nothing, no warning at all, which seemed odd. Painfully, I struggled to my feet and the other soldier got to his one good foot.

After we started off again, a big Sherman tank came along and stopped to give us a ride. The top of the tank was already crowded with wounded men, but the driver said to climb on, if we could find room. Some of the guys scooted aside and reached to help us up. It was much better than trying to get my buddy to the aid station on foot. That was my first time to ride on a tank.

Nightmare to Nightingale

The tank carried us the remaining distance to the makeshift aid station. There we saw scores of other wounded soldiers awaiting attention from the medics. As the wounded were helped off the tank, the more serious ones were given prompt emergency treatment as needed. The others of us just found a place wherever possible to sit on the ground until a medic was available. The field aid station was a crude half shelter, hastily erected along the side of the road. It was stocked with minimal facilities for the purpose of temporary aid only, to sustain the wounded for the longer ride to the field hospital. At length, two of the medics were freed up enough to just bind my arm close to my body so that it could not move or be jostled. They made sure the bleeding had stopped before loading me onto a jeep sometime that night.

The jeep ambulance took me to an enormous tent serving as the field hospital. In that location, personnel and equipment was available for more involved procedures and surgical operations. As I was carried into the big tent on a stretcher, I could see men on stretchers spread out, filling a wide area. My stretcher joined the others on the dirt floor of the tent. Then I was finally allowed to rest peacefully and a welcome sleep overtook me.

With the constant stream of wounded coming in, it was necessary for the doctors and medics to work in shifts around the clock every day, for as long as the battle lasted. Sometime during the night a doctor awakened me and said it was my turn.

I replied, "Doctor, there are many others here in worse condition than me. I am resting good and have no pain. You could take some of them, and I can wait." He said, "But it is your turn! We're taking you now."

At that, two aides picked up my stretcher and carried me into the main field hospital tent. Rows of tables were there already occupied by other soldiers. I was placed on an empty one, and they wasted no time. My shirt was removed, a needle was stuck into my arm, and I was told to start counting. I can remember starting to count, 1, 2, 3, 4, 5...6.....7......... then I was completely out!

I awoke to something amazingly dreamlike, yet it was real! It was the most exhilarating experience in all of my travels overseas. I was in a soft bed, not a foxhole. My left arm and chest were securely encased in a cast. Standing before me was a very beautiful young nurse, holding a plate of food and ready to feed me. It was unbelievable!! What a far cry from sitting in a foxhole eating field rations! I could have easily used my good right arm to feed myself but I wasn't about to tell that to the pretty nurse. I enjoyed every minute of the pampering, the food and the presence of that nurse with her comforting smile.

The next meal was something of a letdown though. I still got the plate of good food, but there was no sight of the beautiful young nurse carrying the tray. I suspect she was in big demand, trying to brighten the spirits of other guys as they awakened from surgery. It wasn't long until I was moved to a large overcrowded holding tent that was jammed with wounded soldiers who had been treated. Every one of us would be shipped out, but some were ready before others.

While waiting to be shipped out, I reflected upon the chaplain who had spoken to us and had prayed with us when we first landed on Okinawa. His exact words escape me after all this time, but I clearly recall that he stressed the importance of trusting in a living God who holds our destiny in His hands. He told us that we may not understand why God would allow this conflict, but we knew the purpose of engaging in it was to protect the freedom of our country, the United States of America, from the hands of adversaries and evil people.

He encouraged us to hold fast to our faith and that God would go with us as we went into battle. He asked that God would have a place in Heaven for any of us who had a bullet come our way with our name on it! That prayer was very meaningful to all of us. It was especially a blessing to me because of my belief in the redeeming qualities and mercies of God our Savior. Although the chaplain's message was probably a consolation to most of the guys, it really seemed like he thought he could pray everyone into Heaven, regardless of their knowledge of salvation and commitment to the Lord. Yet in my heart, I understood that a person needed to confess his sins to the

Lord and accept Jesus as his Savior to be accepted into the kingdom of God.

Nevertheless, his admonition was well taken and no doubt it helped many of the men to pray. It was my prayer that those who were not saved would feel the need and take that opportunity to pray personally to be accepted by God. Also, I prayed for protection. My prayer was that even if I were to be wounded, I would not come face to face with an enemy in such a way that I would have to kill him. Yet, we were conditioned to do just that! If the enemy was coming our way we knew full well it was kill or be killed. My prayers were answered! God did protect me in His own way. Yes, I was shot and wounded. Piercing my left shoulder, that bullet was entirely too close to my heart for comfort. While harming me, it took me out of greater harm's way. For that, I have ever since been grateful!

Looking around in that crowded holding tent, it was obvious there were soldiers with much more serious wounds than mine. One soldier had his eyes bandaged and was asking the doctor if he would ever see again. There were internal injuries, legs amputated, head injuries, and many other conditions too numerous to mention. A man nearby required abdominal surgery. One had a leg bandaged and was crying for pain relief. I began praying for those guys, for my friend Herbert, and all those soldiers who were still fighting their way from hilltop to hilltop to win the Battle of Okinawa.

It was plain to see, from looking around, what Tokyo Rose meant when she broadcast about the blood of Americans being found on the hills of Okinawa. Tokyo Rose was the Japanese radio propaganda personality Japan used in an attempt to break the American soldiers' morale. She often spoke about current combat engagements with pointed accuracy. Around that time she broadcast this message: "Sugar Loaf Hill, ...Chocolate Drop, ...Strawberry Hill.

Gee, those places sound wonderful! You can just see the candy cane houses with the white picket fences around them, and the candy canes hanging from the trees, their red and white stripes glistening in the sun. But the only thing red about those places is the blood of Americans....only those who've been there know what they're really like." I had heard her on Saipan and again in one of the tent cities on Okinawa.

A hospital ship eventually took most of the wounded from Okinawa to a hospital on Guam, Saipan, or Hawaii. I was assigned as a *litter* patient to be evacuated by plane because the hospital ship was overcrowded. When it came time to leave the hospital tent, about 10 of us were loaded onto the back of an army truck on our stretchers and taken on a very rough ride to the airfield. The stretchers were just flat on the bare metal floor. That was probably the most excruciating ordeal thus far. Even the hard cast could not prevent the jolting of my wound. From the moans and cries of the others, I knew it was even more painful for those in worse condition than me. The army had no fancy easy riding ambulances on the island. It was a matter of getting us out of there quickly with the trucks that were available.

We were loaded onto a plane especially equipped for patients on stretchers. It had special shelves to carry 50 stretchers. I would have rather been put on the hospital ship, because it was the first time in my life that I had ever flown on an airplane and I had a bit of anxiety about it. I guess that seems ironic after having lived through the dangers of the front lines of battle, but the butterflies were real, nonetheless. The thought of getting there faster helped to alleviate my fears.

The plane's destination was Guam. Guam had been taken by the U.S. Army and Marines a few months earlier in a fierce battle similar to that of Okinawa and other islands of the Pacific. Guam is a neighbor island to Saipan. It is a part of the chain of the Mariana Islands. Once there I was taken to a military hospital where I was treated quite royally. The attendants did everything they could to make me comfortable. I was given a private room and served good meals.

They also provided me with pen and paper so that I could write a letter to my family. I wanted to get a letter sent right away because I knew they would be worried about me. I had not written for over two weeks and they probably thought that I was still on Okinawa. Since boot camp, up until I went to the front, I had usually sent a letter home each week. I would regularly get a reply from somebody at home. However, some of the mail that they sent to me while I was overseas never did catch up with me. I let the family know in my letter that I had been wounded in the shoulder, but I was now safe from harm and getting excellent care. They received the letter just a few days before I got home.

After two days in the luxury of a private room, I was put on another plane and sent to Hawaii. In the hospital there, I was assigned to a large room with several other recuperating soldiers. Two of them were strung up with some kind of traction. On the following day, a couple of Red Cross ladies came in with a New Testament for each of us and other small items like a toothbrush, toothpaste, shaving lotion, razor, a comb and a few candy treats. The Red Cross ladies also brought good cheer and made us feel important. I was especially glad for the New Testament. It was a keen reminder again of how the Lord had richly blessed me. I wanted to tell the world about that and yet there was a hesitancy to say much. Would it sound like I was boasting that God loved me better? Or would it sound like a bid for sympathy? I wanted to make neither impression!

While in that hospital, there were motherly-type women volunteers dressed in gray, the men nicknamed them the "gray ladies". The gray ladies would come each morning and massage the arms and back of the bed patients. One day an army officer came striding into the room and proceeded to walk up to my bed. I wondered why he was there to see me. To my surprise he reached out and pinned a medal on my pajama top! He had just presented me with the *Purple Heart Medal,* which was given to soldiers wounded in battle. It was such a surprise, because I had never heard about the medal.

The following day, I was taken for an x-ray and a new cast put on. They gave me a uniform and assigned me to a ward with several guys in it. I could now go to the cafeteria for meals. And what meals they were!!

We were served buffet-style with what seemed to be every kind of food imaginable. We could have anything we wanted and as much as we could eat at every meal (and no KP duty)! There were no complaints from the men during that time. However, it just seemed so unfair for us to be feasting while those other guys in our division were still over there in Okinawa living in foxholes, fighting from hill to hill, risking their lives to secure the island. I wondered if perhaps they had taken Mount Shuri and the Shuri Castle by that time, which was the objective of the 77th Division. We knew only too well the horrible things they faced and here we were living in luxury! I thought perhaps the rationale was that the wounded had paid their dues and now deserved honorable treatment.

Some of the guys with lesser handicaps were permitted to get passes to go to town or elsewhere on the island. Upon their return, we heard seemingly wild stories about the excitement in town and what a wonderful place it was. I surmised from their tales that the beautiful trees and surroundings at the hospital facility was all I really cared to see of the island. My condition probably would have allowed me to go out somewhere, but I just had no desire to leave the comfortable surroundings and good meals right where I was at.

Homeward Bound

I was in that hospital ward for about two weeks. It was quite a rowdy place. The recuperating guys were not much inclined to anything spiritual. So I found private moments in the evening to read my New Testament and pray. I gave thanks to Jesus for saving me twice…first eternal salvation and now leading me safely through so many trials thus far. Life was pleasant and leisurely there, but I was glad to hear my name called when it was time to prepare for being shipped out.

Several of us were loaded onto a bus and taken to the docks to board a large ship, which carried both civilian and military passengers. Four of us, with similar injuries, were assigned to a stateroom on the main deck. Several other soldiers were on the ship, but we were not permitted to walk about and mingle. We were not allowed to go anywhere except the small deck just outside of our room. From there, we could see nothing but water. All of our meals during the four-day trip were brought to our room, because we could not leave that room. I wonder if that may have been for the purpose of keeping the soldiers from getting too rowdy.

I do not regret fulfilling my duty to go to war. I came home safely. However, on the battlefront it had been an eerie feeling to wonder when and how a bullet or explosion might come my way. As I reflect back on my military experience, it could be considered a blessing in disguise. It was a firsthand education of what war is really like. It enables me to deeply empathize with those soldiers who are at war now or at any time, after having been there myself. I also had the opportunity to make new friends and explore unusual places that I would otherwise never have seen.

The Walls Came Tumbling Down

While I was on Okinawa, it was known that Shuri Castle lay ahead of us on top of Mount Shuri and was considered the headquarters of the Japanese army. The extent of the network of caves under Mount Shuri, that the Japanese were using, was completely unknown to the Americans.

Shuri Castle, sitting atop Mount Shuri, was the location of a difficult battle toward the end of May. Historians had described Shuri Castle as one of the most magnificent castle sites to be found anywhere in the world. Records are not available to make clear as to just when Shuri Castle was first built. Most sources claim it was built during 1237-1248 before the island of Okinawa was divided into three kingdoms–two centuries before it was organized into a unified monarchy.

The castle had been burned to the ground during disputes over the kingdom of the Ryukyu Islands, which included Okinawa in the 1450s. It was rebuilt with further embellishments and expanded during the reign of King Sho Shin in 1477-1526. This later construction included stone dragon pillars and other architectural refinements as well. Through the medieval and early modern periods the residents of Shuri were primarily those associated with the royal court. It continued to be a prestigious place of residence into the 20th century.

The Japanese forces seized Shuri Castle in 1609 and restored King Sho Nei to his throne, giving the castle and the city to the Okinawans. Records indicate that the castle was rebuilt in 1672 following a fire in 1660. At that time the roofs were tiled to make them more fireproof, as they had been previously covered with wooden shingles. The castle burned and was rebuilt again in 1690, 1709, and again in 1730. The kingdom was a vassal state to Japan for 250 years.

In the late 19th century, the kingdom of Shuri was abolished when Japanese Imperial forces proceeded to the castle and presented formal papers of Tokyo's decision to occupy the castle with a Japanese garrison and the main gates were sealed. The castle, along with the nearby mansions of former court nobles, fell into disrepair during the ensuing years; the Japanese garrison neglected maintenance of the premises. The lives of the aristocrats were shattered as well and Shuri shrank in population and importance.

The garrison was removed from Shuri in 1896 and three years later Shuri Ward petitioned the national government of Japan to convert the grounds into a leisure space because the Okinawa Prefecture had not provided funds for maintenance and public leisure space. The petition noted that it would be most regrettable if the castle were to sink into further disrepair and dilapidation due to abandonment. The Ward requested ownership of the grounds, but was denied. Finally, Shuri Ward was permitted to buy the land outright in 1909 and proceeded to repair and maintain the castle. Pressure to restore, conserve and protect the historical sites of Shuri began in 1910. The castle was converted into an Okinawan shrine in 1925 and declared a National Treasure in 1928.

Shuri Castle

The Japanese again took control of Shuri Castle when they moved in to build the entire island into a fortress of defense against the anticipated eventual invasion by the United States. A major military command post was hidden below the castle in caves, but the castle itself was being used as a fortress by the Japanese troops when it was under attack by the Americans.

On May 29, just 12 days after I left the front, the First Marine Division and the 77th Army Infantry (of which I had been a part) were beginning another assault on Shuri. That was part of the U.S. Tenth Army's offensive against the Japanese defenses centered on Shuri Castle. By the end of May, *Operation Iceberg* was two months old and badly bogged down. The fast-paced opening of the campaign to seize the island had been replaced by week after week of costly exhausting attrition warfare. The 77th Infantry Division and the First Marine Division had advanced barely 1,000 yards over several days, gaining only a little ground each day. They maneuvered over one honeycombed ridge after another with reverse slope canyons. Each division was on the side of the long Shuri Ridge, which was the nerve center of the Japanese army. This was the outpost of dozens of their forward artillery observers, who had made life so miserable for American assault forces all month long. Of course, that was their objective.

The American generals called upon nearby battleships to fire upon the castle to eliminate and destroy the hundreds of enemy troops holed up there. However, unknown to the Americans, most of the Japanese had already left Shuri by night and escaped. The Battleship USS *Mississippi*, the oldest of the U.S. battleships, fired thousands of 14-inch rounds on Shuri Castle, totally destroying it. The *Mississippi* was later hit by Japanese kamikaze bombs and severely damaged. The attack also caused a dozen casualties and the death of the captain.

Battleship *Mississippi* [Source: Wikipedia]

But the *Mississippi* did not lose power and had maintained firing power from some of its guns. It was still in the area to accompany the Battleship *Missouri* and other ships to the Japanese harbor for the signing of the terms of surrender, which took place later in the year.

On the rainy morning of May 29, it was said that things seemed different and quieter. American forces had overrun both the east and west outposts of the Shuri line. The castle seemed no longer invincible. As the armies converged upon Shuri, they were expecting the usual firestorm from the Japanese troops. But there was none the Marines reached the crest of Shuri Ridge with hardly a firefight.

The company commander of the Marines looked west a few hundred yards and saw the ruins of Shuri Castle. The medieval fortress of the Ryukuan kings was there for the taking. Everyone had expected the Japs to defend it to the death, regardless of the bombardment! In actuality that is just what they had done! All the troops holed up there had been killed. The place seemed lightly held with only distant small arms fire. Field radios buzzed with the astonishing news!

Advance by 77th Infantry Division on
Shuri Castle, Okinawa
[Source: AC40 Photos at pbase.com]

Since it lay beyond their boundaries, the Marine Corps asked permission to seize the prize, but their commander, Major General Pedro del Valle, refused their advance. He knew that by all rights the castle belonged to the 77th Division, who had fought so fiercely for it and had called for their support. He recognized that it would not be fair to grab the Tenth Army's objective. Del Valle gave the Army's General Bruce of the 77th, the go ahead. The Tenth Army's Company A swept west along the ridge and took possession of the battered complex. Only then did the 77th Division witness the destruction resulting from their call for a major bombardment of the castle.

One of the Shuri Castle bells

The bombardment and destruction of the castle killed all Japanese soldiers that remained after 70,000 had escaped into the three tiered caves below and to other positions south of the castle. The only remains of the castle were two large bronze tattered bells that had withstood the bombardment. Enemy corpses lay in piles, again giving off an unbearable, putrid stench. The nauseating smell of decomposing bodies indicated many had been killed several days before the capture with neither time nor place to bury them. In addition, hundreds more dead Japanese were found in the almost 2,000 feet of the subterranean network under the castle. Those caves, some large enough for trucks and other equipment, had been dug the hard way by pick and shovel. Much of it was apparently done by enslaved Okinawan people in the months before the American invasion.

Seizing Shuri Castle represented a definite milestone in the Okinawa campaign, but it was not the victory. The flag raising on Mount Shuri (at the castle site) was not the end of the battle, as was the flag raising on Iwo Jima a few months previously. The brutal fight on Okinawa would go on for another twenty-four more days. After the war, the grounds around Shuri lay in ruins for decades. In 1992, the castle was rebuilt attempting to follow the original design, but even more majestic. The surrounding area, called Shuri Park, was declared a World Heritage site in the year 2000. Today, Shuri Castle is a famous tourist site visited by thousands each year.

The Battle of Okinawa ended approximately one month after I left the island. The records say the last battle was fought on Hill 89, where many men, of both armies, lost their lives. Most of the Japanese who were not killed in the battle committed suicide to avoid being taken prisoner. They would have considered defeat as a humiliating and unbearable disgrace.

It was reported that some of the surviving Japanese officers and soldiers knew that the war was lost. The reason given for agreeing that it was the end of the war for Japan, was that they realized that they could not hold out indefinitely against such a formidable force as the United States.

The following statistics can be found in the many writings available on the history of the Battle of Okinawa. The Americans suffered over 62,000 casualties, of which over 12,000 were fatal. This number included over 4,900 sailors who lost their lives during the eighty-two day battle. The U.S. Navy suffered a greater loss than in any other battle. Thirty-six ships were sunk and 386 were damaged. Most of the damage was done by the suicidal pilots of the kamikaze planes and ships. Seven hundred sixty-five U.S. aircraft were lost.

Over 107,000 Japanese soldiers were killed. Some 20,000 were sealed in caves. An unusually large number of Japanese soldiers (7,400) were actually willing to lose face, surrender, and be taken prisoner. It required a large compound to hold so many. It was highly unusual to take so many prisoners. The Japanese authorities indoctrinated the Okinawans also to believe that suicide was more honorable than to be taken prisoner. It was a rare thing for a soldier in the Japanese forces to surrender. Local Okinawans, who had been conscripted by the Japanese army and did not accept the "no surrender" way of thinking, accounted for many of those who did surrender.

It is reported that at the end of the battle, a final count of known names of U.S. service men, Japanese soldiers, and civilians killed on Okinawa amounted to 402,208 people. It has been estimated that up to as many as 50,000 names were unaccounted for.

The people of Okinawa had been fed Japanese wartime propaganda which caused unwarranted fears. This explained their initial resistance and a large number of suicides. Many Okinawans thought they were fighting for their lives against "barbarous" Americans. Once the civilians and even many Japanese soldiers, began to learn that the American troops did not intend to hurt them, they began surrendering. They started coming to the Americans in droves, giving themselves up in a submissive manner. The survivors learned they had been given false information. Not only was the report of American "savagery" incorrect, on the contrary, part of the intricate plan for the U.S. invasion of the island included bringing enough food and supplies to feed them!

The Okinawans who had been living in caves were terrified to come out after the fighting stopped. Seventy-five percent of their homes had been destroyed. They were unbathed, starved, and injured from bombing, shelling, and bullets.

A very disturbing story surfaced regarding the civilian Student Corps of Nurses. Intensive nurse's training had begun in 1944. Students from the Okinawan Girls School and the Okinawan Normal School made up the Himeyuri Student Corps composed of school girls. These were the most well-regarded girls in Okinawa. When the battle began, roughly 225 of these girls (ranging in age from 15 to 18) were conscripted to serve as nurse aids in the Japanese military hospital.

The hospital was located underground in the caves. The treatment of these young ladies was despicable. They were required to do the most menial and dangerous work. Some even faced danger by attending to wounded soldiers in the battlefield. Others were even forced to serve as *comfort women.*

By the latter part of May 1945, the Japanese had lost 75 percent of their forces stationed on Okinawa. They abandoned Shuri and headed south. The military also abandoned the young women. The medical units were deactivated and the girls were forced out of the caves. They were left to their own devices and moved south, unprepared and unprotected. One of the classmates explained the situation, "One after another they died in vain, attempting to find safety and family." By the end of June only 21 of the over 200 remained alive. [Source: Laura Lacy]

The last battle for the Sixth Marine Division on Okinawa occurred on June 17, 1945. The United States flag was raised on the southern end by the Sixth Marine Division on June 21, by the same outfit that raised the flag on the northern end. Fighting stopped on July 2, 1945, at which time the island of Okinawa was declared secure.

Surrender marking the end of World War II came aboard the U.S.S. Missouri in Tokyo Bay, on Sept. 2, 1945. Gen. of the Army Douglas MacArthur, far left, signed for the Allies. Gen. Yoshijiro Umezu signed for the Japanese army.

The signing of the terms of surrender took place on September 2, 1945, on the deck of the Battleship USS *Missouri*.

Over 90 percent of all buildings on the island of Okinawa were destroyed. Most farmlands were littered with the machinery of war or torn up to such an extent that they could not produce food. It is estimated that between 50,000 and 150,000 native Okinawans died, which was nearly one third of the total population of 500,000. Some historians record that over 10,000 Okinawans committed suicide because Japanese soldiers encouraged them to kill themselves rather than be taken by the "ruthless" American soldiers. Many were given hand grenades with which to blow themselves up before being captured. Some went to a high cliff and threw their children and themselves over to their death. Others were sealed in caves where they had taken refuge with Japanese soldiers.

169

Hundreds of books, articles, and papers have been written about the Battle of Okinawa, which Winston Churchill called, "among the most intense and famous in military history." The United States claimed that it was the costliest battle in the Pacific in terms of both lives and material.

The senior Japanese officer, Yahara Hiromichi, in charge of military operations in Okinawa, escaped from the last battle by disguising himself as a teacher. He was later recognized and taken prisoner. Later in life, Hiromichi published a book about the battle on Okinawa from his point of view. He spoke of the many Japanese soldiers committing suicide on Hill 89, where the last battle was fought, rather than surrender. It was his claim that he and two other senior officers remained on the hill ready to commit hara-kiri (cutting one's abdomen open, the national form of honorable suicide). According to Hiromichi, they reasoned among themselves that one of them ought to live to tell the story of the Battle of Okinawa. He volunteered to stay alive, even at the cost of the dishonor it would bring upon him. This was the reason Hiromichi gave for trying to escape, rather than surrender. The other two high-ranking officers took their own lives there on that hill.

Hiromichi stated that he had realized the Japanese were defeated on the first day of the American invasion. He said he had three reasons for holding out and refusing to surrender. First, it would be an unpardonable dishonor to the Emperor of Japan. He might even be dishonored to the extent of being executed in some dishonorable manner. Secondly, as previously mentioned, prolonging the battle there would give more time to prepare for the American invasion of their homeland. Third, he wanted the American army to pay the highest possible price in loss of lives and all our resources for the possession of Okinawa. His pride and loyalty to Hirohito, the Japanese Emperor, cost the lives of over 350,000 people and the almost total destruction of Okinawa.

Our own officers predicted that an invasion of Japan would have cost over one million lives. The Japanese claimed that it would have been suicidal for the Americans to attack Japan, because they had thousands of kamikaze crafts ready and capable of sinking all the American ships that came close to the mainland. If they had sunk the majority of our ships, thousands of American Naval sailors, Marines, and U.S. Army personnel would have been sent to the bottom of the sea.

CHAPTER SIX

GOD BLESS AMERICA!

Recuperation and Restoration

The Army hospitals were crowded places during World War II as is the case in any war. While at a hospital in Hawaii, such as this, was where an officer came and issued the *Purple Heart* award to those of us who were new arrivals.

I t was a blessed feeling to be back in the U.S.A. We were all transported to a large U.S. Army hospital in San Francisco for a short three-day visit and checkup.

A Red Cross volunteer came on one of those days and selected three of us for a grand tour of the city. During the tour, I could see that the city of San Francisco looked entirely different than it had on our previous visit (on our way to the war). The man took us to a high elevation where we could overlook the vast sweep of houses in a densely populated part of the city. I had never known there was such a large area of houses. At the end of the tour he took us to a fish vendor near the seashore where he purchased some crabs. I was curious how he was going to prepare those things because I had never seen anyone fix crabs to eat. We didn't know we were to be enlightened before the day was done. He had planned a surprise crab feast at his home before taking us back to the hospital. His wife welcomed us into their home and treated us as if we were children of her own. She dressed the crabs and served us a delicious seafood dinner along with other dishes she had prepared for that occasion. Cake for dessert was the finishing touch. It was her way of showing her appreciation to us. The crabmeat was almost as good as the turtle that we caught in the abandoned Wabash and Erie Canal, back home in Indiana.

From San Francisco I was transported by train to a large recuperation and rehabilitation hospital in Nashville, Tennessee. As before, I enjoyed traveling by train and observing the scenery across the United States. What a far cry from the battlefield! A different world!

The hospital in Nashville was expressly for soldiers who were not seriously injured and were expected to serve again. Those of us there knew well that our next deployment would likely be to take part in the invasion of Japan. That is what we were trained and prepared for. What we did not know was, the Japanese were preparing to sink our transport ships with thousands of kamikaze bombs. I would hope, even now, that our military leaders knew of their plans and were preparing to eliminate them before the troop ships arrived to the area.

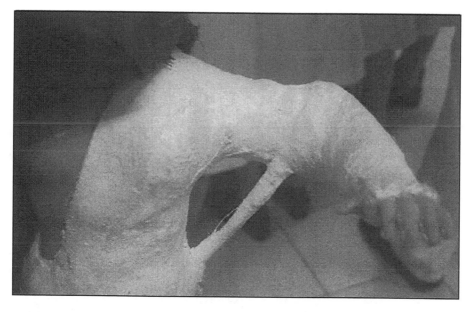

This is the type of body cast that I wore all the way from Okinawa by plane to Hawaii, by boat to California, by train to Nashville, and then home. It had been replaced at Hawaii and again at Nashville.

One morning my cast was removed and left off for several hours. While I was without the cast my arm seemed perfectly well, with no pain or impairment. I was hoping that would be the end of having to wear it, but later in the afternoon I was called back into the doctor's office where another similar cast was put on.

Shortly afterwards, I was given leave and travel vouchers to Princeton, Indiana, with orders to return in 20 days. I called home that evening to let the family know what time someone should meet me at the Princeton train station the next morning. What a joyful surprise to see not one or two, but four of my family there to greet me! I immediately spotted Mom standing on the platform, anxiously watching for me to get off the train. There she stood with my sister Lelah, Wayne (Lelah's husband), and my younger brother Morris. At first, Mom did not recognize me because I was wearing a body cast and a garrison cap. When she did recognize me, she ran to hug me with tears of joy. She wrapped her arms around my neck, thankful to have me safely home again. Then she quickly released me thinking she might hurt my wound. There was no chance of that, wrapped up as I was in the strong cast. Feeling the loving arms of my mom around me was the best welcome I could ever have had!

It was a little awkward at first. The others seemed rather spellbound or perhaps it was just reluctance to ask questions. They knew I had just returned from a long and perilous journey. We hardly knew how to make conversation. It was as if they were concerned that they might say something offensive about my condition. They were probably astonished at seeing my body cast.

To put them at ease I purposely chatted with a cheerful countenance and this simple explanation, "Don't fret about me or my condition. I'm just glad to be home. I feel good and am in no pain except for the discomfort of this body cast. I may try to take it off when we get to the house. I know you are anxious to know where I have been." I went on to tell them how happy I was to see them all and how wonderful it was to be back home.

Immediately Mom began to object about me removing the body cast. She questioned, "Are you sure your wound is well enough for that? You might get in trouble if you take it off or hurt it. Or you might cause it not to heal right!"

I explained, "The cast was removed at the hospital and left off for several hours. Then they called me back and put on this new one. I'm sure that I can take care not to hurt the arm."

Seeing and being near them again was pure joy. The warmth of family love filled the car as we drove the familiar roads from Princeton to Clark's Station. Half an hour later we turned off the highway onto the rock road, which led to our house. There, just before the old canal and railroad, we pulled in the drive and I was home. Orace Wayne (my youngest brother), watching for the car, was next to join the celebration!

Thinking about the effect the cast would have when meeting other relatives, friends, and the congregation at church, made me distinctly uncomfortable. I would have to make the same explanations repeatedly. I did not want sympathy or to appear as a hero, so I asked the boys to help me remove the cast. Mom renewed her objection to that and the boys were reluctant to do it. Having experienced moving around comfortably without the cast while at the hospital, I knew I would be careful and be just fine without it. I assured them that my wound was well and that it would be okay to remove it.

The boys were glad to help out with that! They got knives and began cutting slits in the cast down my arm and along the right side, while being very careful not to cut too deeply. I had full trust in their skills with a knife. Mom could not watch for fear that the knife would slip and cut the wrong thing. I had no fear of that! She fretted so much over their work that she had to go do something else while the boys were performing the "operation". Once they had it cut through, they carefully spread the cast open and away from my body and arm. They all got a good look at my scar on my shoulder and back to see how close it came to being a fatal wound. The bullet had come within inches of my heart!

When Pop came home from work he was glad to see me. We had never been much on hugging in our family but he eagerly shook my hand and expressed his relief to see me home. In the course of conversation, I began to learn how much they had fretted about me. They had been terribly worried during the time of not getting any correspondence from me. They knew I had been in the battle on Okinawa, and were continually worried about my safety. The news over the air waves and in newspapers was not comforting. It kept people somewhat informed about the progress of the war, but no one could really know what it was like without being there. The notice from the U.S. War Department actually arrived, to tell them I had been wounded in battle, while I was home! They were a little late! I was glad to have been there in person to give firsthand information to the family. That saved them added worry.

Morris and Imel were glad to furnish transportation for me. It was a blessing to be able to attend my regular church again and be with all the good people there. They were holding a revival. The folks at church would have liked to have heard about the war and my travels, but I was not much of a talker and probably disappointed them by not having much to say about my experiences.

Some friends and relatives tended to honor me or stand in awe, for where I had been and what happened. I know they felt special recognition was due, but that was rather uncomfortable for me. I usually responded to any such expression with a word of thanks to the Lord for my deliverance from the battlefield, and that the real heroes are the many who did not return. At that time Okinawa had been secured, but I still did not realize the extent of lost lives.

Everywhere there were signs of relief from the austerity that had prevailed during the height of the war, when everything was in short supply and items were rationed. I visited with neighbors and got caught up on the local news. It was summertime and the Pike County Fair was in full swing. Some of the family and I attended one evening. Besides the entertainment, the county fair was always a good place to see familiar faces. All too soon, my leave was over and it was time to return to Nashville. Twenty days can go by very fast sometimes. Nonetheless, being back with the home folks in my own "stomping grounds" had been a real blessing. Now it was time to return to Nashville and probably on to Japan. Not a word was said about my missing cast when I returned to the hospital.

"Never Surrender" Surrendered

One morning, shortly after arriving back in Nashville, the headline news in the paper read: ATOM BOMB DROPPED ON HIROSHIMA. The bomb was dropped on August 6, 1945. With no response from the Japanese toward surrender, another A-bomb was dropped on Nagasaki, Japan three days later. That was astonishing news to the whole country! It was hard to imagine that one bomb could destroy a whole city. Still we had no definite assurance that the war was over. Even though leaflets had been dropped at the time of the bombing, urging Japan to surrender to avoid further disaster, they had not yet offered to surrender!

President Truman made a special radio report to the nation, after the bombing of Hiroshima, announcing the use of the new weapon. He stated to the United States, "We may be grateful to Providence" that the German atomic bomb project had failed, and that the United States and its allies had "spent two billion dollars on the greatest scientific gamble in history and won."

Just one atom bomb was more destructive to Japan than many other conventional bombs

After the second bomb on Nagasaki, President Truman expressed these words to our nation, "I realize the tragic significance of the atomic bomb. It is an awful responsibility that has come upon us... We thank God that it has come to us, instead of our enemies, and we pray that He may guide us to use it in His way and for His purposes."

President Harry Truman 1945-1952

It is recorded that President Truman met with military leaders and other government officials to discuss the use of the Atom Bomb. After much deliberation the ultimate difficult decision rested with Truman. He claimed it was not an easy or hasty decision...the parties involved knew that both sides of the conflict would lose many more lives with an invasion of Japan.

A different announcement was made as a warning intended to Japan, "If they do not accept our terms of surrender, they may expect a rain of ruin from the air, the like of which has never been seen on this earth. Behind this air attack will follow sea and land forces in such numbers and powers they have not yet seen and with the fighting skill, of which they are already aware."

It was reported that the Japanese warlords called a meeting immediately thereafter. For the first time in Japan's history, the Emperor, Hirohito, met with his military leaders. He urged them to surrender to the United States, rather than have their country totally destroyed. Japanese officials partially justified to the Japanese public their decision to surrender on the fact that the Soviet Union had launched an invasion on Manchuria, and declared war on Japan. They had enemies on all sides and no remaining allies. Yet, a few leaders wanted to hold out, thinking they could defeat their enemy on the homeland.

Within a few days, in newspapers around the world large headlines read: JAPAN SURRENDERS! That was good news to the whole country and especially to all of us recuperating there in the hospital!! That meant we would not have to return for the invasion of Japan, which would have cost the lives of thousands more American young men!

When that news was announced there was great celebration in downtown Nashville and in cities all over the United States. However, no patients at the military hospital were permitted to attend any celebrations. Not even those who were ambulatory or fully recuperated. But, we celebrated in our hearts and among ourselves! The next morning we read all about the revelry and celebrations in the newspaper. It was big news! Everyone wanted to get their hands on a newspaper.

In Japan it was quite a different story. The whole country was humiliated over the capitulation and surrender. Because of what they had started, many thousands were killed. Because of their culture of kamikaze and die before surrender, many thousands of others were suffering from the effects of the atomic bombs.

Had Imperial Headquarters of Japan not accepted the terms of surrender, another atomic bomb was scheduled for August 19, upon the approval of President Truman. Other bombs were also being readied and decisions being made as to where to drop them.

Back to Base

Within a week, after my return to the hospital in Nashville, some of us were ordered to report to San Antonio, Texas, for reassignment to active military duty. It was a relief to know the war was over and our next assignment would be in the United States, not back into battle. I was given travel money and allowed 15 days to get to San Antonio. That was just enough time for another short visit home. To conserve the travel money,

I took the bus to Petersburg rather than the train. Instead of calling ahead as I had before, I took the family by surprise that time. I was with them a couple of days, during which I got a map to plan my route to Texas. The family gave me a good send off on my 1,000 mile journey to San Antonio. Mom packed some food for me to take along.

I had decided to hitchhike. That again allowed me to save quite a bit of the money which had been supplied by the military. It was very easy for soldiers to get a ride without much waiting. I was experienced at catching rides from the time when I was at Purdue University. I had learned some good techniques to use when thumbing for a ride. I would always dress respectably, hold out my thumb and wear a friendly smile. The only payment necessary was conversation and a word of thanks. It took just a couple of days for me to get to San Antonio!

Upon arriving at the Army base in San Antonio, I was assigned to a processing center where there were at least a hundred other soldiers also waiting for reassignment orders. My time there was about to offer me some interesting experiences that I had not really anticipated. Never being one to enjoy sitting around loafing or playing cards, I was anxious to explore the city or find something to do. I liked the location and hoped some officer would ask for a volunteer for something, thinking I might get assigned to that base. But, we had no choice in our assignments.

Herbert Weithorn married to Gladys Glieber
April 26, 1947

As soon as possible I called the home of my friend, Herbert Weithorn, in McGregor, Texas. I was eager to learn what had happened to him. His mother answered the phone and gave me some unexpectedly good news.

She told me that not only was Herbert okay, he was in San Antonio! To my further surprise, I learned he was in the rehabilitation center right there at the same camp where I was at the moment. I was anxious to get some free time so I could go see him. The processing routine seemed to crawl as I proceeded through it.

As soon as I could get away I found Herbert, in the rehab center, getting therapy in the use of his injured hand. What a grand reunion! Of course, he was astonished to see me. He said that ever since the time I was shot he wondered what had happened to me. We swapped stories and got caught up. He described how his hand had gotten shot while he was merely fixing his poncho over his foxhole. He went on to tell me that he was sitting in his foxhole looking directly at me and saw me get hit. He told how I spun around and fell to the ground. He had been quite concerned about how seriously I may have been wounded. He also told me the horrible news about our platoon sergeant. He said that the next day after I left, the sergeant was shot right between the eyes!

We went on to share other memories of our travels and of those terrible days on the hills of Okinawa. We talked of the long march to the front lines, being in the foxholes, bullets flying around us, and the many other experiences that we had been through on Okinawa. Our talks were part of the healing process. There were things we could say to each other, that just were not possible for others to understand unless they had been through the horrors of combat. It meant so much to both of us to see each other again!

A Pig and a Chicken

Herbert mentioned that there was to be a big community *Texas style* barbecue on that upcoming Saturday. His family and others nearby were putting it on. He invited me to come to his house Friday evening, stay the night, and attend the barbecue the next day with him. That was just the kind of adventure I was looking for. I was able to get a weekend pass from headquarters, and Friday afternoon I hitchhiked the 175 miles to McGregor. When I got in town I called Herbert's home and someone came for me in a pickup truck. Herbert was with friends and not home yet. His mother made me feel so welcome, showing how very glad she was to meet me. She sat me right down to a delicious meal, far more than I could eat. She was very gracious to me in every way, and was just so happy to meet someone who had shared time in the war with her son. I'll never forget the royal reception of Mrs. Weithorn. She treated me like I was one of her own children.

The next day Herbert gave me the grand tour. We drove around their farm, through the community and into the "big" town of McGregor (population 200). He explained their farming procedures and other things that were quite different from the way it was in Indiana. It seemed that everything there was done on a much grander scale.

In the afternoon the tour concluded at the home of his neighbor, who was hosting the big barbecue.

The men were cooking three hogs on a grill, over an open pit of burning coals. The hogs had been split in half and had been cooking slowly for 24 hours. A marvelous aroma filled the air. While the meat was cooking, it was basted with a barbecue sauce that was an old favorite recipe made by Herbert's mother. The women were busy preparing other foods and deserts.

In the evening, the pork was ready to be sliced. It was served along with homemade bread and the other wonderfully prepared food to eat. At least 100 people attended the feast. That stands out as the best barbecue that I recall having ever eaten. Herbert's family and friends graciously welcomed me.

The food was excellent and the evening enjoyable until I learned about Herbert's undisclosed plans for me! He had made some secret plans for later that evening, after the barbecue. He may have suspected I would have balked had I known in advance. He said there were two girls needing an escort home. One girl was Herbert's date. The other girl was set up as a blind date for me! I went along with the game, but felt very uncomfortable. I was too backward to enjoy being thrown into the company of a girl I didn't know. I was tongue-tied and felt so awkward trying to talk to a female stranger. It had been no problem talking to and becoming acquainted with hundreds of strangers in the army, but this was a girl! The proverbial "cat" certainly had my tongue, and I did not shine as "Mr. Personality".

She must surely have thought I was a real dud. When we finally got to her house, I did manage to walk her to the door and say *goodnight*. I hadn't attempted to hold her hand or anything. What a relief to get back in the car and to the safety of Herb's house. The next morning, after Herbert's mother fixed us a good hearty breakfast, one of his friends drove both of us back to the camp in San Antonio. The weekend with Herbert had been a real nice time…all except the short-lived date!

Among the many interesting men I met at that replacement center in San Antonio, was a soldier who had endured the unbelievable horrors of the Bataan Death March. He was one of the few who survived it.

He related to me some horrifically inhuman, cruel things he had witnessed and personally experienced. Soldiers, captured by the Japanese, were forcibly marched mile after mile over a period of three days; it was hours on end without rest and given no water. Those who became exhausted and dropped out of line, even to get a drink, were immediately shot, stabbed to death, or beheaded.

Riding horseback, alongside the prisoners, were Japanese officers carrying large swords. As they rode the line, occasionally they would swing that heavy sword and simply cut off the head of a man who seemed very weak. You never knew if it was going to be your head when they approached.

Some of the Japanese officers rode horseback alongside the American and Philippine prisoners on the 60-mile torturous Bataan Death March.

American and Philippine prisoners who survived the march were required to slave long hours on a starvation diet. Soldiers and other prisoners of the Japanese endured the most horrible kinds of torture imaginable. If anyone thinks the atom bomb should not have been dropped, they should take the time to get an educated opinion, by reading or hearing of the atrocities and torturous life that people suffered under the domination of the Japanese.

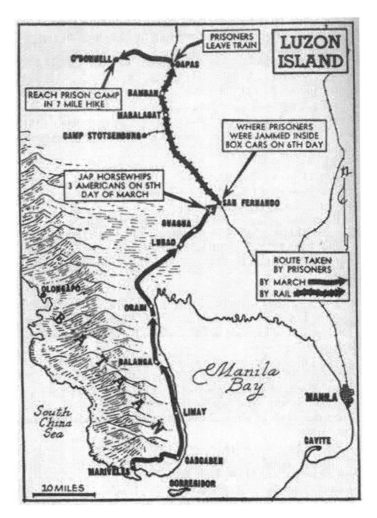

Map of the 60-mile Bataan Death March

Another soldier in the barracks, there in San Antonio, was a particularly friendly person named Thomas. After we became acquainted, Tom invited me to go with him to visit his girlfriend, who lived in a small town about 60 miles from camp. She had a sister who would also enjoy spending the afternoon with us. At least the double date was not a surprise sprung on me, like what had happened while visiting Herbert. I was feeling a little more brave the second time around, also it seemed better than loafing around camp all weekend.

My new friend advised me that I needed a better pair of shoes than army boots for the arranged date. One evening, he took me to a place he knew in town where I could buy a nice pair of shoes. Encouraged by Tom, I splurged on a pair of Florsheim shoes! I had never paid so much for shoes. They were $10! Those were very expensive shoes for the times. One could get an ordinary pair of shoes for around $4.

On Sunday morning we hitchhiked the 60 miles to the town where the girls lived. Even as two fellows hitchhiking together, we made good time and got there around noon. We finally found the girls' apartment, but were not invited in. That probably would not have been proper and actually, we preferred to wait outside anyway. After we stood around for half an hour, the girls made their grand appearance. Both were very attractive and obviously had taken pains to look their very best. Tom's girlfriend was probably 19 years old and her sister was just a little younger. I thought it would be inappropriate to actually inquire about their ages.

This time I attempted to be a little more conversational and courteous, while still keeping it on just a friendly basis. Both of the girls complimented my exceptionally shiny shoes. Did they suspect I had purchased them especially for that occasion? They were obviously brand new. Altogether, it was an interesting afternoon with Tom's girlfriend being our tour guide. She directed us past their church and other sights, where we might see and, more importantly, be seen. We strolled through the park, stopped at an ice cream stand and rested on a park bench. It was a pleasant, relaxing afternoon, and I appreciated that they had chosen the outdoor atmosphere rather than sitting awkwardly in someone's parlor. After about four hours we escorted the girls back to their apartment and bid our farewells. Then we caught the first ride going back to camp and made good time.

Dreary, Desolate Destination

A few days later I received my orders for an assignment to the Army Ground Forces at Fort Bragg, North Carolina. That time I was able to tell Herbert where I was going and promised to stay in touch. During all of our travels, we had unexpectedly made contact despite the odds against some of those reunions. I had no doubt that I'd be seeing my good friend again someday.

I boarded a train bound for Fort Bragg with a feeling of anticipation. Even though each change of location took me to another unknown, there were new things to see and do. Little did I know I was headed across the country to my final military duty station…and an important destiny in my life.

It was a chilly night in October of 1945 when I, along with the other soldiers assigned to Fort Bragg, arrived in

Fayetteville, North Carolina. An army vehicle awaited us there to transport soldiers to the camp, which lay about 10 miles from the train station. Being nighttime made it difficult to gain much of an impression about what the place was like. It was a state that I knew practically nothing about, nor did I expect to be there long enough to become very well acquainted with the area. I well knew that I could expect to be abruptly sent away, anywhere at any time. That did not add any cheer or enthusiasm. As for North Carolina, I was not even aware that I had been sent very near the home of my immigrant ancestors. My family line of Willis's had migrated to the *New World* from Wales to this area. My lack of interest was about to be turned around!

During the time of WWII, a variety of ground force operations and training were conducted at Ft. Bragg. The base also maintained strong air force training. After the war, I was assigned to the Army Ground Forces here.

A disappointing breakfast the next morning seemed to go right along with my attitude about the place. We had such delicious meals in other locations, but this one ranked especially bad. Upon leaving the mess hall, full but not happy, I began to consider how I might make the best of the remainder of the day. I was not yet on the duty roster. The idea of returning to the barracks or visiting the recreation room was a dreary thought. That sort of non-activity quickly became very monotonous to me. All I could think of was taking a walk around the base to explore whatever I could.

It was completely unimpressive. Beyond the barracks I saw only scrubby oaks, scraggly pines, and barren white sand. What a forlorn and desolate place to be sent! The barracks were fine, but the food was about the worst that I had experienced in the army. Maybe the royal treatment I had received, while in the hospitals and other places I had been during my recuperation, tainted my opinion after being treated so well. I decided I detested the place and hoped that I could leave as soon as possible. The base was not a good representation of the state. I had just not seen the real beauty of North Carolina yet!

CHAPTER SEVEN

THE FLOWER OF FAYETTEVILLE

Heels to Wheels!

A couple of days after arriving at Fort Bragg, I was instructed to report to the company office for duty assignment. The officer in charge wondered why I had been on base for two days and had not reported for duty. I actually should have done that the first day of my arrival but I was depending on the company sergeant to tell me those things, as was his job. Fortunately, my explanation for attempting to get word from the sergeant on duty seemed acceptable to him.

I was assigned to the Army Ground Forces Testing Unit. I was not told anything about the job and had no idea what we were supposed to be testing or why. I was not looking forward to it and liked it even less when it began. I followed orders, which was typical of the military, whether they made sense to us or not. Instructions were few and explanations even fewer. It seemed like it was something just to keep me busy. It was better in some ways, than other meaningless or more rigorous jobs that I had previously been on but I was still not happy with that assignment and just went through the motions of what I was told to do without any sense of accomplishment. A few days later the captain in charge of the operation realized that I was not the right person to be on that job. Based upon his recommendation, I was soon transferred to the mail department in the large Ground Forces Headquarters building. That job entailed hand-delivering and receiving mail, as well as various other documents around the many offices within the building. Fort Bragg now began to be a little more acceptable. The job was interesting and I thought it was important. It was something that was necessary, which made me feel that my time wasn't being wasted on just busy work.

The officers were all very friendly and would often want to chat a little about my Okinawa experiences. A few would take notice that I wore the Purple Heart bar among the other decoration badges on my shirt.

When I was off duty, I was not the type to sit around in the barracks or the smoke filled day-room where many guys liked to relax and pass the time playing cards, shooting pool, and loafing. A few times, on Saturdays, we were furnished transportation to the golf course on base. It was a free activity, so six of us took advantage of it one day. Having never played the game, I tried it that one time. I could see I didn't care for golf enough to go back. At least it was something wholesome and an outdoor activity. But none the less, I have never been interested enough to play golf again.

Mine, in Time

Probably the best recreation offer given to us was the free bus service into the city of Fayetteville. I took advantage of that every weekend, when not on duty. I located a Church of God in the town to attend on Sundays. The worship services were good and there was an added sparkle to them. A very pretty girl sang in the choir and since she was up front I could easily adore her! After church, I usually stayed in town for the evening service. In between services I loafed at the USO or other places of interest. I liked to stroll around Fayetteville on Sunday afternoons, after having lunch somewhere. The Cape Fear River ran through the city. I learned that it had a lot of history surrounding it and began to locate other historical places throughout the city. I especially liked to go to the river bridge and join others there, just watching the peaceful flow of the water and the occasional log or other piece of debris floating away.

Cape Fear River Bridge

On the second or third time I went to the church, during Sunday school class "the girl" and I sat close to one another and we exchanged glances. I learned her name was Berline Barefoot and she worked at Rose's Five and Ten Cent Store after school on weekdays and Saturdays. That was the most important thing I learned in Sunday School that day! From that time on, things really started looking up around Fort Bragg.

Rose's Five and Dime has become a department store

I began finding opportunities to visit Rose's Five and Dime. Fayetteville had suddenly become a very interesting city!

I was now able to see the beautiful pines, instead of just scrub oak. The white sand was good to walk in and my work at the fort became interesting. Even the food was good and I enjoyed the barracks better. It was amazing how everything had improved in such a short time!

Berline Mae Barefoot - 1945
North Carolina Southern Belle

Sometimes I would go to town on Saturday, since I could spend the night at the USO and be there bright and early for church the next morning. One morning at the USO, I woke up and found to my great dismay that someone had stolen my beautiful shiny new Florsheims. There in their place sat a sad looking bedraggled pair of old shoes that looked like they had waltzed across Texas and back! I went to a shoe store to find replacements, but I sure didn't want to spend $10 again. I settled for something decent, but more normal in price.

At the USO I met another soldier who was there, like me, just to get away from camp for an interesting walk or other activity to help pass the time. He suggested we go to the roller skating rink, which was just eight blocks from the USO. I had never had on a pair of roller skates, but had done plenty of ice skating on the canal by my boyhood home. With the usual reluctance that accompanies the first time of doing something, I agreed to give it a try. After adapting to the difference between blade and roller, I found I enjoyed it as much as ice skating.

The Post Delivery Corporal received his discharge from the military three weeks after I had been assigned to the Ground Forces headquarters pager job. Being next in line, I was in the right place at the right time to move into his position. When I was given his position, it included a promotion to Corporal.

WWII U.S. Army Jeep like I used to
deliver mail all over Fort Bragg in 1946

That job involved the delivery of mail and documents
all over the post. What freedom! It was a responsible
job and coupled with the freedom of movement around
the base, made the job a most interesting one. To my
delight, a jeep was even furnished for my use. Soon I
became acquainted with all of Fort Bragg. The base
actually began to take on a new interest to me. There
were even times when deliveries had to be made outside
the base to the Army Air Force base. While there, I
could watch the big planes coming and going. My days
at Fort Bragg had become something to look forward to.

One day I was faced with a dilemma. A tire was going down on the jeep. I made it to the motor pool before it went completely flat. The guys there announced that it was my job to fix my own flat tire! I knew how to do that okay. The problem was, I had on my dress clothes, which were required for the delivery position. Not seeing any solution, I figured I might just as well ask for some tools and get it fixed, if that was the way it was to be. Soiled clothes could always go to the laundry! However, I realized I would soon be expected back at headquarters for other possible deliveries. I decided it would be best to notify the boss at the office. Going into the motor pool office, I called and explained the situation. The captain said, "Let me speak to someone there."

I handed the phone over to a person sitting nearby, who appeared to be in charge of the motor pool. He was given strict orders from my captain to fix that tire immediately or let me have another jeep. He told the guy that I had deliveries to make, and left him in no doubt that it was their place, not mine, to fix flat tires. The workers jacked up the jeep and in short order had replaced the wheel.

Promotion to Sergeant

I held that satisfying position a few weeks, then the headquarters mail sergeant, who sorted the mail, received his discharge. Again, I was promoted in rank, this time to Tech Sergeant and subsequently, advanced to the position of Mail Sergeant. The promotion gave me a little increase in pay. It was interesting work but it cut in on my freedom of movement. That job was to sort all the regular mail received at headquarters, which I liked, but I did miss driving all over the post in the little jeep. It was not long until the Staff Sergeant, who sorted the classified mail and directed it to the proper departments, was moved to another position. I was again promoted in position and rank to Tech Staff Sergeant.

It was then I received news that Mom's cousin, Bertha Gilliland, had passed away. I was given an emergency leave of 10 days to attend the funeral. I hitchhiked home, but when it came time for me to report back for duty I had a ride the entire way. My brother, Morris, drove me back to North Carolina. Thirteen-year-old Gerald Gene Gray, my sister's (Marybelle) son, went along for a lark. It was a long 24-hour drive, but we could drive straight through by taking turns driving. The three of us enjoyed the drive through the Smokey Mountains, which were so amazing. Compared to the hills of Indiana, they were enormous.

Before leaving Fayetteville, Morris and Gerald Gene had a chance to meet the special acquaintance I had made while attending the Church of God. After meeting Berline, they drove me back to my barracks that night and then immediately headed back to Indiana.

Upon my return to the barracks, the first thing I heard from the guys was, "Willis, you're getting discharged! You start mustering out tomorrow!"

What wonderful news! Berline and I had continued seeing one another and had discussed what we would do when this time arrived. We realized we were in love and had made some plans. Three other soldiers were assigned to travel with me by train to Camp Atterbury in Indiana for our discharge. There we would receive our final discharge procedures. I was the highest ranking soldier, so I would be carrying the travel orders including the train tickets and meal vouchers. My discharge from the U.S. Army was received on June 6, 1946. Three hundred dollars was my mustering out pay, plus I had accumulated a savings of $900. That amounted to what seemed like a healthy sum at the time.

All discharged personnel were furnished transportation to their choice of destination. I chose my destination to go only as far as Indianapolis, Indiana. From there I was a free man! On my own! This time I didn't hitchhike home. I had enough money to purchase a car. At a used car dealer in Indianapolis, I bought a good used 1939 Buick that had only one previous owner. It looked to be in good condition (inside and out) and the motor seemed to run very well. Of all things, it even had turn signals, which I had never seen on any automobile. What a thrill to be free and driving home to Clark's Station in my own prized possession!

1939 Buick - like the first car I owned

In great anticipation, I thought about what a surprise it was going to be to my family, not only seeing me back so soon, but pulling in the driveway in my fine used Buick! I was not disappointed. It truly was a happy surprise and wonderful reunion with everyone. Oh, how I enjoyed showing off my car to my family! This time there was no cloud hovering over us because I would not be leaving again for the service. I was a different man now, than when I set off on my military journey. I had been through a lot, both good and bad. Now it was time to collect my thoughts and do some serious planning for my future.

My reason for purchasing a car so quickly was that I would need transportation to North Carolina to bring back my special sweetheart, beautiful Berline! Before I left Fort Bragg we had become engaged to be married. I spent a few days at home, which included some correspondence with my fiancée by letter. Then, Morris returned with me to Fayetteville where Berline Barefoot and I were married on July 5, 1946.

Our Home in Bloomington, Indiana

We returned to Indiana, where I would attend college to continue my education. We built our small home in Bloomington, near Indiana University. Our first two children, Bonnie Mae and Hervey James, were born in our new home.

James and Berline - their first winter together
Bloomington, Indiana 1946

In three years I finished my Bachelor's Degree in Education, which allowed me to get a teacher's license in 1949. I then started my career teaching there in Monroe County. I was able to complete my Master's Degree in School Administration during the next three years. That was accomplished by taking night classes and summer school while teaching in the day. During those years our third child, Patricia Lou, was born.

After receiving my Master's Degree in 1952, we moved to southern Indiana, where I worked for six years in teaching and administrative positions. In the ensuing years, two more children, Alvin Eugene and Barbara DeAnn, were added to our family. Our family of five children was complete.

Together, we have enjoyed many happy experiences in our various activities of working, playing, and traveling as a family. Most of the growing up years of our children were spent at our country home, which we bought near a small community just eight miles southwest of Petersburg. We called it *Whip-Poor-Will Hill*. While living there, we regularly attended the Church of God in Petersburg. Our entire family holds fond memories of that special time in our lives.

My retirement in 1988 ended my full-time teaching career. We sold our home at Whip-Poor-Will Hill and moved to Indianapolis in 1997. We wanted to be closer to our three children who were living there. Berline also retired from her nursing career, but we both remained active and productive in various ways and jobs. She could spend more time growing her many varieties of flowers and helping others of the family with their children and projects. We also spent three years adding some space on to our new home. It was not in our vocabulary to be idle. I found that I enjoyed semi-retirement by doing part-time substitute teaching.

It has been a joy to share my teaching and life experience with a new generation of Americans. The Lord has blessed us with a successful family and many good years together. To God be the glory!

[A.E. Willis Illustration]

CHAPTER EIGHT

OCCUPATION AND RECONSTRUCTION

The surrender of Japan ended the four terrible long years of WWII. Actually, the seeds of World War II began years earlier when Hitler rose to power in Germany and Japan invaded China. The United States was also involved in an indirect way prior to 1941, by aiding Great Britain with war machinery and supplies in their defense against German expansion.

The years leading up to and including WWII brought untold inconveniences, hardships, and suffering to innumerable people in most parts of the world and death to millions. Aside from suffering the loss of so many loved ones, the rationing of food and inaccessibility of goods–the U.S. began to experience economic prosperity. It had been necessary for the U.S. to gear up quickly for mass production of machines of war such as airplanes, tanks, ships, weapons, and other materials. Automobile companies discontinued making civilian vehicles, during those years, and shifted to making war machinery. An infinite number of other war supplies and products had to be put on assembly lines all over the nation. We were not reliant upon other countries to supply us with everything, as is happening today! To the contrary, factories were busy in the United States. That resulted in well-paying jobs for many and a general economic boom for our country. Many people gained a better life economically, good positions, and even wealth in some cases. How ironic that prosperity was a byproduct of the war, at the expense of so many giving their lives for our freedom. War, however, isn't fair.

The United States had a total of 16.5 million people who served in the military during the war; there were over one million casualties, of which 416,000 died. Most of the other major countries involved suffered far more casualties. Archives of the war claim that a total of more than 20 million people perished during that war, not counting the millions that died in the systematic slaughter of Jews during the German Holocaust.

No doubt the cost of planes, ships, and other equipment lost, as a result of the war, ran into the trillions. I also doubt there could even be a close estimate of the cost of property damage, nor the number of civilian deaths.

A period of occupation of the defeated countries followed the end of the war, especially Germany and Japan. The occupation of Germany was divided into four sections, each of which would be occupied by one of the four main Allies: United States, Russia, England, and France. Japan was occupied by the United States under the leadership of General MacArthur, the commander of the Tenth Army throughout the war in the Pacific.

The United States assumed responsibility for the stability and reconstruction of Okinawa and other islands of the Pacific. Okinawa was in shambles and the United States furnished materials for reconstruction. They oversaw the replacement of buildings, construction of roads, and restoration of the land into production. Okinawa, today, scarcely resembles the country it was before the war.

General MacArthur took charge of the occupation of Japan immediately after the official signing of the surrender terms. The minesweepers and underwater demolition teams first moved into Tokyo Bay to make it safe for shipping vessels. (A minesweeper was a ship used for dragging a harbor or an area of the sea in order to remove, disarm, or harmlessly explode mines laid by an enemy.) After that, Marines and Infantry units came ashore, making the landing in full battle gear, prepared for any treachery from the Japanese.

The first order of business was to release all POW's the Japanese were holding and give them immediate medical attention. The condition of those individuals must have been a pitiful sight to see. Treatment in the Japanese prisoner of war camps was inhumane. In fact, a very large number of American prisoners did not survive it.

After the *all clear* was given and with no further Japanese resistance, it was deemed safe for all units to arrive and take charge of the country.

Photos: Coast Guard, U.S. Navy

THE WAR IN THE PACIFIC

Pouring into Peleliu. A wave of Alligators, tough little cannon-carrying tanks that fight on land or water, churns toward the beach on Peleliu Island to storm the Japanese defenses. The landing-craft ship from which the Alligators were launched sends a protecting barrage of rocket fire toward the enemy on the coast.

Blasting Guam. A Marine howitzer, the short, powerful cannon that accounted for many Japs, goes into action shortly after the American invasion of Guam.

Taking Tinian. Marines wade ashore to the beach on Tinian Island, bound for the fighting front inland. Their landing craft may be seen in the background.

Landing on Leyte. Landing craft of all sizes unload fighting men and supplies after the invasion of Leyte. This was the first island to be taken from the Japanese in the long campaign to liberate the Philippines.

[The World Book Encyclopedia, 1958]

General MacArthur flew to Japan and set up the Supreme Allied Headquarters in Yokohama. Additional Marine and Army forces arrived over the next several days.

By the end of 1945, over 250,000 U.S. personnel were in Japan. The government of Japan was changed to a democracy, which was the minimum goal of *the occupation*. Gradually, the U.S. forces were reduced until the occupation of Japan officially ended in 1952. Full occupation of Okinawa continued until 1972.

Atomic Bomb. Smoke towered 20,000 feet above Nagasaki, three minutes after the atomic bomb struck.   Manila Sound. Japanese envoys at Ie Shima on their way to discuss terms with General MacArthur.

[The World Book Encyclopedia, 1958]

The B-29 named Enola Gay dropped the atomic bomb that destroyed Hiroshima. A second atomic bomb destroyed Nagasaki, after the Japanese refused to surrender. The bombs averted an all-out invasion of Japan. It is regrettable that it was deemed necessary to drop *any* bombs on innocent people anywhere in the world.

JAPANESE SURRENDER

The U.S.S. *Missouri*, a 45,000-ton battleship from which Admiral William F. Halsey commanded the victorious Pacific Fleet, was designated by President Truman as the scene of the first Japanese surrender in modern history. The *Missouri* was anchored in Tokyo Bay for the ceremonies, held on September 2, 1945. High officers of the Allied nations took part.

General MacArthur Speaks. After formal announcement of Japan's surrender, General Douglas MacArthur spoke to the Allied officers assembled on the main deck of the U.S.S. *Missouri*.

Japan Surrenders. Japanese Foreign Minister Shigemitsu signs the surrender document on board the *Missouri*. General MacArthur, standing near table, looks on.

"So Sorry!" Former Japanese guards at the notorious Ofuna prison camp near Yokohama bow low as their American prisoners leave after the surrender of Japan.

Ruined Yokohama. This heap of rubble was once a thriving business section of Japan's fifth largest city. It was destroyed by incendiary bombs from United States planes.

[The World Book Encyclopedia, 1958]

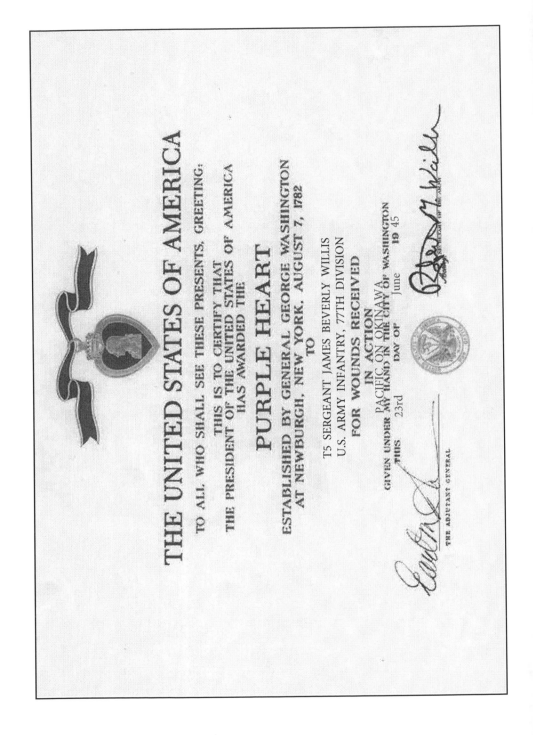

CONCLUSION

It is my hope that this soldier's personal experience has enabled the reader to gain a better understanding of what it was like to serve in World War II and the way America responded to foreign attack at that time. It is desired that this volume may be a resource for students of American history. My personal account is, herein, added to numerous others already on record, in the attempt to preserve the history and significance of the forced struggle and violent fighting for every yard of earth slowly gained and the critical and complex decisions necessitated by that massive war.

It is important to future generations, when this one is gone, to learn from eyewitness accounts of the sacrifices made, so those who are privileged to live in freedom will understand that it must be guarded, and sometimes preserved through battle. Those who participated in World War II, were there by necessity. In doing so, we had to fight our worst fears and, in many cases, call upon the Lord of the universe for protection. Reading historical accounts, such as contained herein, should impress upon citizens, young and old, that in the end, doing the right thing does matter! Decisions and choices we make affect our freedom and our destiny.

This book is dedicated to all veterans who have sacrificed to serve their country. May learning from the past be a deterrent to complacency and impart courage to continue upholding freedom. May Americans appreciate and preserve the precious gift of *life, liberty, and the pursuit of happiness*, which God has given this nation. As the United States of America faces threats at home and abroad, let us "humble our hearts, turn from our wicked ways, and repent," so that God will continue to bless America.

II Chronicles 7:14

A CHANGE OF HEART

God has allowed me to live beyond the tragedy of war for such a time as this. I have been eternally thankful for His protection and have tried to be faithful to live for Him throughout my life. Eternal life is far greater than time spent on this earth because heaven is forever and ever.

How do I get there? Well, there is only one way. In John 14:6 Jesus said, "I am the way, the truth, and the life. No one comes to the Father except through me."

Just call out to Him with a humble heart and say, "Lord Jesus, please forgive me of all my sins and come in and change my heart and life. Thank you for loving me enough to lay down your life for me and dying on that rugged cross.

I accept your precious blood was shed for me and washes me clean of every sin. I believe you rose from the dead and you are alive today. Thank you for giving me eternal life and filling my heart with your peace and joy. Thank you for coming into my heart. I accept you as my Savior and Lord now and forever. Amen."

If you have prayed this salvation prayer from your heart, the Lord has heard and all the angels rejoice for you because your name has just been written in the Lamb's Book of Life! God speaks through His written word. It's like a roadmap–showing you the way. Read the Bible for it will lead you into all truth!

SOURCES

Abrams, *Front Page*, A collection of Historical Headlines from the Los Angeles Times, 1987

A.E. Willis, Illustrated Drawings

Lasky, Lisa, Photo of Herbert Weithorn

Lacy, Laura, *Battle of Okinawa*, 2004

Leach, Paul, *77th Division History*

Powell, Anita, photographs

United States Military Archives

Wikipedia (the Free Encyclopedia)

World Book Encyclopedia, 1958, 1963

Yahara, Colonel Hiromichi, *The Battle for Okinawa*

Author's Note

A followup book is being prepared as a more complete memoir of my life. It is to include not only the years before and after my war experience, but also the heritage of my family ancestors, who migrated from England to North Carolina and eventually settled in Southern Indiana.

Hopefully, the reader will find this publication an interesting and informative story.

To purchase additional copies of this book:

www.indianamilitaryveteran.ecrater.com

Craigslist.org

Ebay.com

createspace.com/4452665

To contact the Author:

James Willis

PO Box 39512

Indianapolis, IN 46239

317-495-2958

Made in the USA
San Bernardino, CA
13 October 2015